DATE DUE

OCT 1 5 2014		

Lyme Disease

Titles in the Diseases and Disorders series include:

DISEASES & DISORDERS

Lyme Disease

Shannon Kelly

LUCENT BOOKS
A part of Gale, Cengage Learning

GALE
CENGAGE Learning

Detroit • New York • San Francisco • New Haven, Conn • Waterville, Maine • London

GALE
CENGAGE Learning

LIBRARY OF CONGRESS CATALOGING-IN-PUBLICATION DATA

Kelly, Shannon, 1970-
Lyme disease / by Shannon Kelly.
   p. cm. -- (Diseases & disorders)
Summary: "This series objectively and thoughtfully explores topics of medical importance. Books include sections on a description of the disease or disorder and how it affects the body, as well as diagnosis and treatment of the condition"-- Provided by publisher.
Includes bibliographical references and index.
ISBN 978-1-4205-0635-8 (hardback)
1. Lyme disease--Juvenile literature. I. Title.
RC155.5.K45 2011
616.9'246--dc22

2011006375

Lucent Books
27500 Drake Rd.
Farmington Hills, MI 48331

ISBN-13: 978-1-4205-0635-8
ISBN-10: 1-4205-0635-8

Printed in the United States of America
1 2 3 4 5 6 7 15 14 13 12 11

Printed by Bang Printing, Brainerd, MN, 1st Ptg., 06/2011

Table of Contents

"The Most Difficult Puzzles Ever Devised"

Charles Best, one of the pioneers in the search for a cure for diabetes, once explained what it is about medical research that intrigued him so. "It's not just the gratification of knowing one is helping people," he confided, "although that probably is a more heroic and selfless motivation. Those feelings may enter in, but truly, what I find best is the feeling of going toe to toe with nature, of trying to solve the most difficult puzzles ever devised. The answers are there somewhere, those keys that will solve the puzzle and make the patient well. But how will those keys be found?"

Since the dawn of civilization, nothing has so puzzled people—and often frightened them, as well—as the onset of illness in a body or mind that had seemed healthy before. A seizure, the inability of a heart to pump, the sudden deterioration of muscle tone in a small child—being unable to reverse such conditions or even to understand why they occur was unspeakably frustrating to healers. Even before there were names for such conditions, even before they were understood at all, each was a reminder of how complex the human body was, and how vulnerable.

While our grappling with understanding diseases has been frustrating at times, it has also provided some of humankind's most heroic accomplishments. Alexander Fleming's accidental discovery in 1928 of a mold that could be turned into penicillin has resulted in the saving of untold millions of lives. The isolation of the enzyme insulin has reversed what was once a death sentence for anyone with diabetes. There have been great strides in combating conditions for which there is not yet a cure, too. Medicines can help AIDS patients live longer, diagnostic tools such as mammography and ultrasounds can help doctors find tumors while they are treatable, and laser surgery techniques have made the most intricate, minute operations routine.

This "toe-to-toe" competition with diseases and disorders is even more remarkable when seen in a historical continuum. An astonishing amount of progress has been made in a very short time. Just two hundred years ago, the existence of germs as a cause of some diseases was unknown. In fact, it was less than 150 years ago that a British surgeon named Joseph Lister had difficulty persuading his fellow doctors that washing their hands before delivering a baby might increase the chances of a healthy delivery (especially if they had just attended to a diseased patient)!

Each book in Lucent's Diseases and Disorders series explores a disease or disorder and the knowledge that has been accumulated (or discarded) by doctors through the years. Each book also examines the tools used for pinpointing a diagnosis, as well as the various means that are used to treat or cure a disease. Finally, new ideas are presented—techniques or medicines that may be on the horizon.

Frustration and disappointment are still part of medicine, for not every disease or condition can be cured or prevented. But the limitations of knowledge are being pushed outward constantly; the "most difficult puzzles ever devised" are finding challengers every day.

Danger in the Woods

"This disease has broken me as far as I can be broken."[1]

These words were spoken by Claire Palermo, a resident of Cortlandt, New York, after she had been struggling for two years with Lyme disease. At age thirty-nine, she was walking with a cane after cycling through a grocery list of symptoms that included rashes, numerous joint pains, insomnia (an inability to sleep), dizziness, fatigue (physical or mental weariness), and irregular heartbeats. By the time she was interviewed by the *New York Times*, she had seen over forty doctors and spent thirty thousand dollars on various medications in an effort to get well. Palermo is one of the hard-luck cases of Lyme: Although many who are treated promptly for the disease respond well and recover quickly—or recover without any treatment at all—others have trouble being properly diagnosed, and some report symptoms that linger for months or even years.

This often confusing and mysterious disease is spread through the bite of ticks, which are bloodsucking arachnids of the arthropod family. They often live in forested areas with dense shrubbery that provides them with a cool, safe environment. Although ticks generally feed on small mammals, birds, deer, and even reptiles, they will also feed on humans if the opportunity presents itself. A hard tick seeks a meal by climbing to the top of a blade of grass or positioning itself on the edge of a leaf and attaching itself to a passing host. Due to this behavior, they are sometimes referred to as "questing" ticks.

If a tick attaches itself to a host and is not discovered, it will feed for several minutes up to several weeks, depending on the type of host, the type of tick, and the tick's life cycle. While the majority of these bites are harmless, some ticks carry harmful bacteria or viruses that can cause illnesses. Examples of these diseases include Rocky Mountain spotted fever, tularemia, babesiosis, and Lyme disease.

Lyme disease is the most common tick-borne illness in North America and Europe and has been found on almost every continent. It has been classified as an emerging disease due to the increasing number of cases seen each year and its geographic spread. Nearly thirty thousand cases were confirmed in the United States in 2009, with another eighty-five hundred categorized as suspected cases. Lyme disease is often misdiagnosed, however, and there are people who are infected and recover without a visit to a doctor. Therefore, many experts believe the true number of cases is probably ten times higher than what is officially recorded. While the greatest concentration of Lyme diagnoses in the United States can be found in the northeastern region of the country, every state except Hawaii has reported at least one case in recent years.

Lyme disease can be a highly controversial topic. Disagreements occur among medical professionals and between doctors and patients on almost every aspect of the illness—transmission, diagnosis, treatment, and long-term effects. For every seemingly true fact uncovered, there is often another one that appears equally believable but completely opposite from the first. A single question can lead to several different answers from several different sources, all of which seem trustworthy. Part of the problem is the nature of the disease itself. Lyme disease has been referred to as the "new great imitator" due to the number of other illnesses it can resemble, making a correct diagnosis difficult at times. Likewise, patients sometimes respond very differently to the accepted methods of treatment for the disease. Author and artist Polly Murray, one of the figures involved in the 1977 discovery of what today is known as Lyme disease, acknowledges the issue in her

Lyme disease-bearing ticks often live in forested areas that provide them with a cool and safe environment.

book *The Widening Circle*: "I am struck by how Lyme disease never seems to act exactly the way it is supposed to, how each individual seems to respond differently to the spirochete [bacteria]."[2] This issue has led to one of the biggest disagreements in the Lyme community: the existence—or not—of chronic (long-lasting or recurring) Lyme disease that resists accepted treatment and requires months or even years of medication to completely erase.

This debate, as well as the rapid rise and spread of Lyme occurrences, will ensure that the disease remains very much in the public eye over the next several years as research on it progresses. It is only in the last few decades that doctors have focused on the condition and it has received much attention and study—the bacterium responsible for causing the disease was not even discovered until 1981. In 1991, Lyme became a nationally reportable disease in the United States, which means that doctors are required to report all cases to their county or state public health department. Other countries have also followed this example. This increased awareness and interest has spurred the search for better methods of preventing Lyme disease in communities, improved tests for diagnosing it, and, perhaps the ultimate goal—a successful vaccine that can prevent it.

CHAPTER ONE

What Is Lyme Disease?

Lyme disease is an illness transmitted by ticks that is considered by most doctors as easy to treat if caught early but that can cause serious problems if left to linger. Although Lyme disease cases have appeared in practically every state in the United States and in many other areas around the world, certain people in certain areas are more likely to be exposed than others. Knowing the facts about the origins of the disease and how it is passed to humans can help explain why this is so and can be useful to health-care professionals in making a correct diagnosis.

Lyme disease is a bacterial illness. Bacteria are single-celled microscopic organisms that can be found in almost every environment on the planet. Most bacteria are harmless—in fact, less than 1 percent of bacteria cause disease. The human body contains hundreds of species of bacteria that usually cause no difficulties and often have useful functions, such as helping in the digestion of food. Some bacteria, however, can cause illnesses. These bacteria are referred to as pathogens, and they can be spread through air, food, water, contaminated soil, or sexual or other close physical contact with an infected person. Other pathogens are spread through the bite of an infected insect such as a flea, mite, or tick. This is the case with Lyme disease, an infection spread by ticks that targets multiple systems of the body.

How Infection Occurs

Lyme disease is classified as a zoonosis—a viral or bacterial disease that can be passed from animals to humans. It is caused by approximately one-third of the members of the bacteria genus *Borrelia* (abbreviated as *B.*), which are members of the spirochete family. Spirochetes are long and slender with a distinctive coiled shape, like a miniature telephone cord. A strain of *Borrelia* known as *B. burgdorferi* sensu stricto is responsible for the majority of Lyme disease cases in the United States, while *B. garinii* and *B. afzelii* account for most European cases. All strains of *Borrelia* that can cause Lyme disease are referred to collectively as *B. burgdorferi* sensu lato. Due to its Latin name, Lyme disease is also sometimes referred to as Lyme borreliosis.

Lyme disease is a vector-borne disease, which means that it is transmitted from one host to another by a vector, or carrier. Although people become infected with *B. burgdorferi* sensu lato bacteria through the bite of a tick, the tick is not

A tick is found on a mouse's neck. Mice, shrews, and chipmunks can carry the bacteria *Borrelia* and any tick that feeds on them becomes infected with the bacteria.

the original host, or reservoir, of the bacteria. Instead, it is the vector. A tick becomes infected with the bacteria when it feeds on a source that naturally carries a Lyme-causing strain of *Borrelia*, such as a chipmunk, shrew, or white-footed mouse. The bacteria then lodges in the intestines of the tick. When the infected tick bites a person and begins to feed, *Borrelia* spirochetes are transferred from the tick's intestines through its saliva and into the person's bloodstream.

There are more than eight hundred species of ticks, but only some of them are known to transmit Lyme. Ticks are divided into two families: hard ticks (Ixodidae) and soft ticks (Argasidae). Hard ticks have, as their name suggests, a hard shield that covers the entire back of the male tick and part of the back of the female. Ticks from this family are responsible for the transmission of Lyme disease to humans. In the eastern United States, the main culprit is the black-legged tick (*Ixodes scapularis*), while in the West it is the western black-legged tick (*Ixodes pacificus*). The eastern black-legged tick is also known as the deer tick, as the deer is one of its major food sources. This is a somewhat misleading name, however, as deer ticks also feed on other mammals and on birds. The main vector in Europe is the castor bean or sheep tick (*Ixodes ricinus*), and in Asia it is the taiga tick (*Ixodes persulcatus*).

Ticks typically come into contact with *B. burgdorferi* sensu lato bacteria before they reach maturity. Ticks emerge from their eggs as larvae. A larva then takes a blood meal from a small host, such as a mouse, which may be infected with the bacteria. After this first meal, a larva will not eat again until it has moved into the next stage in its life cycle: the nymph. Therefore, there is very little chance that a human can become infected with Lyme disease by being bitten by a tick larva. The only way this could occur is if the bacteria had been transmitted from an infected adult tick to its eggs, which is a rare occurrence.

Once it has finished its blood meal, the larva will drop off the host and molt, shedding its skin and developing eight legs. During its nymph stage, a tick may also feed on an infected host (mouse, bird, etc.) or will take a blood meal from a person. This is when ticks are most dangerous to humans. Although adult

Spirochetes

The spirochete family of bacteria is a relatively small one, made up of only six members. A spirochete can range in length from five millionths to several hundred millionths of an inch, depending on its species. Most of them move with the use of a special form of flagella called axial filaments, which are located within the bacterium's cell wall. When the spirochete rotates its axial filaments, it moves in a corkscrew fashion.

Aside from *Borrelia,* two other types of spirochete can cause illness in humans. The first is *Treponema.* The best known of this group, *Treponema pallidum,* is responsible for the sexually transmitted disease syphilis. The *Treponema* bacteria cause sores, and the disease is spread when an uninfected person comes into direct contact with these sores during sexual intercourse. Other *Treponema* spirochetes cause less well-known illnesses such as the skin diseases yaws and pinta.

A type of spirochete known as *Leptospira* causes leptospirosis. Although leptospirosis most commonly occurs in mammals such as rodents, dogs, or livestock, humans can get it by coming into contact with the urine of infected animals. In people it causes fever, chills, vomiting, headache, jaundice, anemia, and sometimes a rash. If untreated, serious kidney damage can occur.

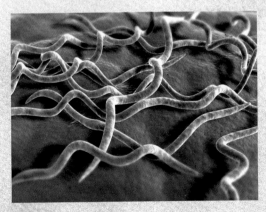

This electron micrograph shows the *Borrelia burgdorferi* bacteria spirochetes that cause Lyme disease in America.

ticks can also transmit *B. burgdorferi* sensu lato bacteria to humans, the adults are more visible to the eye and can be immediately brushed off skin or clothing. In contrast, nymphs are extremely tiny—a black-legged tick nymph is only about the size of a poppy seed or the head of a pin—and their bite is typically painless. A person can easily have a nymph attached to his or her skin and not realize it until several days have passed and the nymph becomes larger due to the blood it has ingested. This is a key issue in the transmission of Lyme disease, as it takes approximately thirty-six to forty-eight hours for the spirochetes to transfer from the tick to its human host. If a tick is removed from the skin before this time period has passed, the likelihood the person will become infected with the Lyme bacteria is relatively low.

Is It Contagious?

According to the Centers for Disease Control and Prevention (CDC), headquartered in Atlanta, Georgia, there is no evidence that Lyme disease can be transmitted from person to person through touching or kissing. The CDC also states that the disease cannot be contracted through sexual contact, although some doctors who treat Lyme patients do not think this is an absolute certainty and believe that further research is needed. One factor that confuses the issue is that the bacterium that causes the sexually transmitted disease syphilis, *Treponema pallidum*, is also a spirochete, like *Borrelia*, so it would seem reasonable that if *Treponema* can be passed through sexual contact, *Borrelia* could be as well. The syphilis bacteria, however, remain close to the surface of the skin in sores, whereas *Borrelia* moves deep into the body.

If a woman contracts Lyme disease during pregnancy and is not properly treated, there is a risk the placenta, the organ in the mother that is attached to the fetus's umbilical cord, could become infected and the fetus could suffer organ damage or be stillborn. In addition, *B. burgdorferi* sensu stricto spirochetes have been discovered in the urine and breast milk of mothers with Lyme disease. In another example of differing opinions

Stamford, Connecticut, health department workers trap deer ticks to test for Lyme disease. Research has revealed the disease may not be spread by sexual contact, but more research is needed to conclusively verify.

in the medical community, while the CDC asserts there are no reports of the disease being transmitted to breast-fed children, well-known Lyme disease specialist Charles Ray Jones, who has treated thousands of children with the condition, claims to know of several babies that he says were infected through breast milk.

Persons undergoing treatment for Lyme disease should not donate blood, as *Borrelia* spirochetes have been found to survive the blood purification process to which donations are subjected. After a person has completed treatment, he or she may be able to donate. Blood banks, however, may require a waiting period after the end date of the treatment or after active symptoms have passed before this is possible. The website for the American Red Cross has a section on infectious diseases under its list of those eligible to donate blood, but Lyme disease is not specifically mentioned.

Dogs, cats, and livestock can contract Lyme disease, but there is no evidence that the disease can spread directly from infected animals to humans. These animals can, however, carry ticks into homes and bring them into contact with humans, so care should be taken to make sure pets are protected with medication and checked often for ticks.

There is no credible evidence that Lyme disease can be transmitted through air, water, or food. Although some animals killed for food, such as squirrels, can be hosts to *B. burgdorferi* sensu lato bacteria, the high temperatures used to cook meat kill the spirochetes. Hunting and dressing game is also not a cause for concern, except that it may put a person in contact with infected ticks in the area.

While *B. burgdorferi* sensu lato spirochetes have been found to exist in mosquitoes and fleas, these insects do not appear to play a role in the transmission of Lyme disease to humans.

Previous infection with Lyme disease does not lead to immunity. People can have Lyme disease multiple times in their life if they are bitten more than once by ticks carrying the bacteria.

Where the Danger Is Greatest

Three major environmental factors that affect whether or not ticks will thrive in a particular area are vegetation, climate, and the availability of a food source. While there is some variation among the habitats of different species of ticks, the majority prefer temperate climates with a constant high humidity at ground level. They are mostly found in deciduous woodlands

Colored scanning electron microscope (SEM) of the head and mouthparts of the deer tick *Ixodes scapularis*, which transmits Lyme disease to humans.

with a covering of litter such as dead leaves or underbrush on the ground. (Deciduous trees are those that shed their leaves seasonally.) Ticks can survive in coniferous forests, however, as long as there is sufficient ground cover and moisture. (Coniferous trees are those that produce cones and have needle-like or scaled leaves.) They can also be found in grassy dune areas, though rarely on open sandy beaches. Areas prone to droughts or flooding are not good environments for ticks.

An ample supply of hosts to feed from must also be present. Again, there is variation depending on the location and type of tick, but the majority of Lyme-carrying species feed from many different sources. In the larval and nymphal stages, ticks tend to feed from birds and rodents such as mice, voles, chipmunks, and rabbits. Adult ticks seek out larger mammals such as deer or livestock. Ticks also feed from reptiles and amphibians such as snakes, lizards, and turtles.

In some cases, the diet of a tick can affect the incidence level of Lyme disease in an area. For example, although western black-legged ticks are numerous in the American West, one of their primary food sources is the western fence lizard, and lizards are not hosts of *B. burgdorferi* sensu lato bacteria. In fact, if a tick that is infected with Lyme disease bites a western fence lizard, the tick itself is cleaned of the bacteria by a protein in the lizard's blood. Scientists believe this could be one reason for the relatively small number of Lyme disease cases reported in the western part of the country. It is also worth noting that although many people associate large deer populations with Lyme disease, deer are actually resistant to Lyme bacteria. The role they play is merely one of providing blood to ticks and, in some occasions, transporting them to new, previously tick-free areas.

Fragmented, patchy forests often have a higher tick concentration than deep, dense woods. One reason for this is that smaller areas of forest—particularly those near human populations—tend to have fewer predator species of animals, which means that small rodents like the white-footed mouse, one of the main food supplies for ticks, can be found in larger numbers. Thus, the suburbs can be just as dangerous as, if not more so than, the wilds of nature. According to microbiologist Alan G. Barbour, "Associating the risk of Lyme disease exclusively with hiking or hunting in the backwoods or wilderness regions is a misconception. Comparatively few people become infected through recreational activities in remote or otherwise unpopulated areas."[3]

High-Incidence Areas

In the United States, there are two major hot spots for Lyme disease: the upper East Coast and a section of the upper Midwest that includes Minnesota and Wisconsin. Infected ticks are also common in some areas of the California and Oregon coastlines. According to data from the CDC, in 2009 the state with the most confirmed cases of Lyme disease was Pennsylvania, with 4,950. New Jersey was close behind with 4,598

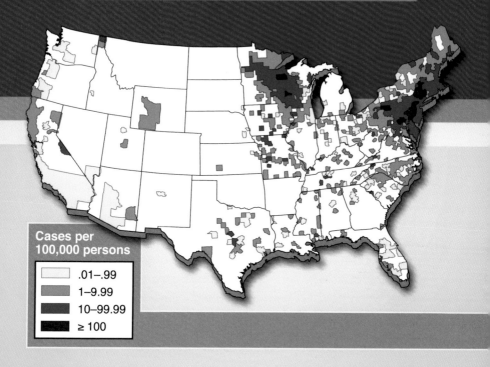

Lyme Disease Incidence by County of Residence—United States, 2003

Cases per 100,000 persons

- .01–.99
- 1–9.99
- 10–99.99
- ≥ 100

Taken from: Centers for Disease Control and Prevention. www.cdc.gov/NCIdod/dvbid/LymeDistribution_Density.html.

confirmed cases, and New York was in third place with 4,134. Up to 50 percent of adult ticks have been found to be infected with *B. burgdorferi* sensu stricto bacteria in the areas of the country that see the most cases.

In Europe, most cases occur in the forested areas of central countries such as Austria, the Czech Republic, Germany, Slovakia, Slovenia, and Switzerland. The number of incidents is poised to increase throughout the continent, however, as recent studies have revealed that significant numbers of ticks examined in other countries are infected with Lyme-causing bacteria. England, Wales, Scotland, and Northern Ireland have all seen an alarming rise in the number of reported cases of Lyme in the last decade. According to the Health Protection

Zoonoses

Zoonoses are diseases that can be passed from animals to humans. They can be caused by bacteria, viruses, parasites, and other disease-causing organisms. The World Health Organization reports that at least two hundred zoonoses have been identified.

The method through which a zoonoses can be transmitted to humas can vary. Some are spread by direct contact with an infected animal, such as being bitten by a dog or bat carrying rabies. Sometimes the feces of an infected animal can contaminate a water supply, and a person who drinks the water falls ill. Other zoonotic agents are spread when a person eats the meat from an infected animal. Tapeworms are contracted this way, as is salmonella. And, as with Lyme disease, some zoonoses are spread when an insect bites an infected animal and then bites a human. Other examples of zoonoses spread in this manner are encephalitis, Rift Valley fever, and the plague.

The treatment of a zoonosis naturally depends on the specific disease the person has caught. Preventive measures include vaccinating animals against zoonotic diseases when possible, thoroughly cooking food before eating, and ensuring a secure and clean water supply.

Some zoonoses are spread when an infected tick or other insect bites a human.

Agency, cases in the United Kingdom have risen by 90 percent since 2006.

In Canada, Lyme disease only became a nationally reportable disease in 2010. This means that all cases of Lyme must be reported to the Canadian public health agency by the medical professionals who diagnose them. The majority of these cases are found in Nova Scotia, New Brunswick, parts of southern and southeastern Quebec, southern and eastern Ontario, southeastern Manitoba, and southern British Columbia. The ticks that transmit the disease in Canada are the same ticks responsible in the United States: the black-legged and western black-legged ticks.

The majority of Lyme cases in Asia are found in the eastern regions such as Russia, Japan, and China. Lyme disease is widespread in China, even in the arid mountain regions of the northeast, and research has shown that migratory birds from that area may have first introduced ticks infected with *B. garinii* to Japan. In Japan, Lyme disease is most endemic—that is, constantly present to a greater degree in that area than in others—in the country's northernmost island, Hokkaido. In Russia, the majority of cases occur in the Ural Mountain region, as well as the northwest and central areas of the country.

Lyme disease is also found in countries in Africa and South America. In Africa, researchers have found strains of *B. burgdorferi* sensu lato, including *B. burgdorferi* sensu stricto and *B. garinii*, in ticks in Tunisia and Morocco, and villages in Senegal, Mali, Mauritania, and Dakar all have reported numerous incidences of Lyme. In South America isolated but increasing cases have been reported in Brazil, Costa Rica, Argentina, and Chile.

In Australia, there is disagreement over whether Lyme disease is present on the continent. Although many people claim to have suffered or to be suffering from the disease, and symptoms consistent with Lyme have been recorded, the government and many medical experts deny it exists in the country. The primary basis for this was a study conducted by researchers from Sydney in the early 1990s in which twelve thousand ticks were collected from the coast of New South Wales and examined. All of the collected ticks were negative for *B. burgdorferi* sensu lato bacteria, as were a limited number of small mammals also tested under the theory they could be reservoir hosts for the spirochetes. Until Lyme-specific bacteria are actually found in a patient, it is unlikely the government will change its position on the issue.

The Life Cycle of a Tick

Regardless of where in the world they are located, ticks that can carry *B. burgdorferi* sensu lato tend to have similar life cycles, and this information can help determine when humans are at the most risk of infection from a bite.

A tick's life has four distinct stages: egg, larval, nymphal, and adult. A female adult tick lays a batch of thousands of eggs in the spring and then dies. The eggs hatch later in the summer into larvae, which have six legs and are extremely tiny—about the size of a period in a newspaper. The activity of larvae reaches its peak in August in the Northeast and upper Midwest regions of the United States. After a larva takes its first (and only, in this stage) blood meal, it molts into a nymph. Nymphs remain inactive during the winter and early spring, emerging to seek the tick's second blood meal in May. Nymphal activity is highest from late May through July in the United States.

After its second blood meal, the nymph molts again and develops into an adult tick, which spends the fall seeking a third and final host from which to feed. The height of adult tick activity in the Lyme disease hot spots in the United States is late October. If the tick is unsuccessful in finding a food source, it will burrow into dead leaves or undergrowth and go inactive through the winter. When temperatures rise above 45°F (7.2°C) in the spring, the tick reemerges to resume its quest for a meal. (It is worth noting that if the temperature rises about 45°F in the winter, ticks can become briefly active then as well.)

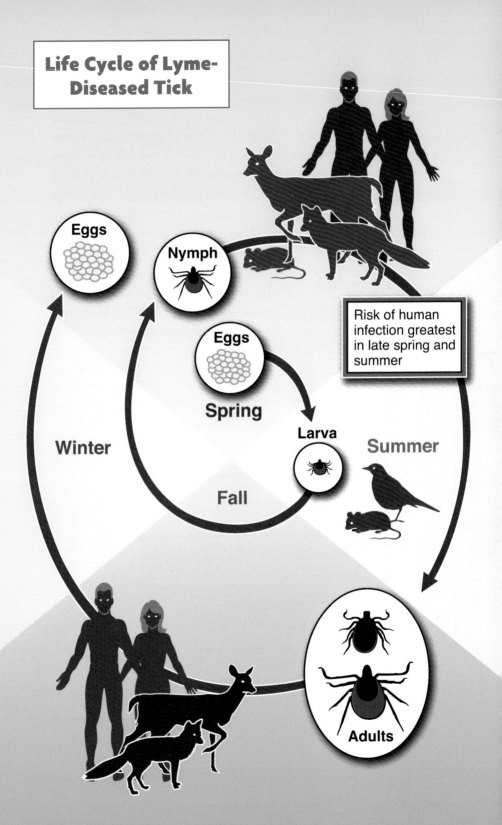

Life Cycle of Lyme-Diseased Tick

Eggs

Nymph

Eggs

Spring

Risk of human infection greatest in late spring and summer

Winter

Larva

Summer

Fall

Adults

For ticks of the Ixodidae family (including the black-legged, castor bean, and taiga ticks), mating is possible only until the adult female finishes her third and final blood meal. Sometimes this mating takes place on the ground, but often it takes place while the female tick is attached to a host. Once mating is complete and the female has taken her last meal, she drops to the ground, lays her eggs, and dies. The male also dies after reproduction. The eggs hatch in the summer and the cycle begins again.

Lyme disease can be contracted any time of the year that ticks are active, but the majority of infections in the United States occur in May through August. Milder and shorter winters in Europe over the last several decades have led to an earlier onset of tick activity in the spring, and most host-seeking activity takes place then and in the early summer, with some areas experiencing another smaller peak in late summer and fall. According to the American Lyme Disease Foundation (ALDF), those most at risk of contracting the disease are people who live or vacation in areas where Lyme disease is widespread, engage in activities or hobbies that put them in contact with overgrown vegetation, work outdoors frequently, and/or do not take the proper precautions to guard against tick bites. Some occupations the organization lists as particularly at risk in areas that report many Lyme cases are landscaping, land surveying, forestry (park and forest rangers), and utility work.

Lyme's Discovery in the United States

In keeping with its reputation as a disease as easily caught in the suburbs as the wilderness, Lyme disease was first officially identified in the United States in the 1970s in the town of Lyme, Connecticut. It began with a local artist named Polly Murray. By 1975 Murray had been suffering for ten years with rashes, headaches, swollen joints, memory loss, nausea, and fatigue. Doctors could find no explanation for these symptoms, eventually informing her that they were psychological,

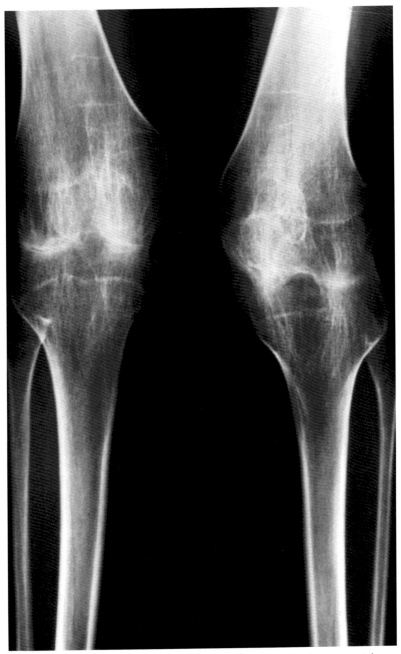

An X-ray of the knees of a patient with juvenile rheumatoid arthritis. The knees show narrowing of joint space due to loss of cartilage.

not physical, in nature. Three of her children were also battling similar symptoms, and one son had been diagnosed with juvenile rheumatoid arthritis, a chronic disease that causes joint pain and swelling in children. Murray began questioning neighbors and discovered that several other children in the town had also been diagnosed with juvenile rheumatoid arthritis. As this is a relatively uncommon disease, Murray found this odd and contacted the Connecticut Department of Public Health.

The health department called upon Allen Steere of Yale University to investigate what was happening in Lyme. Steere was a rheumatologist—a doctor who studies diseases of the joints, bones, and muscles. He determined that the illness was not juvenile rheumatoid arthritis and noted it seemed to strike during certain times of the year and in specific geographic areas in the community. This, along with the rural setting, led him to believe the disease was being transmitted by an arthropod, probably the tick. When it became clear that patients were experiencing more varied symptoms than just swollen joints, what had until then been referred to as Lyme arthritis became known as Lyme disease.

The actual spirochete responsible for Lyme was not discovered until 1981, when microbiologist Willy Burgdorfer at the National Institutes of Health's Rocky Mountain Laboratories in Montana was sent a sample of ticks from the Long Island area of New York State by a colleague. Burgdorfer dissected the ticks and found that 60 percent of them contained a strain of spirochete bacteria in their midguts. Suspecting he had found the cause of Lyme disease, he then set out to fulfill the four conditions used by scientists to determine whether or not a specific disease is caused by a specific bacterium: (1) the bacterium must be present in every case of the disease; (2) the bacterium must be isolated (separated) from the diseased host and grown in pure culture (this means being able to make the isolated bacterium—and only that bacterium—multiply outside the body in a liquid or gel designed to nourish them); (3) when the pure culture of the bacterium is injected back into a healthy host, the host must become infected with that specific disease; and (4) the bacterium must then be isolated from the newly infected host. Tests done using the spirochete met all these conditions and confirmed Burgdorfer's expectation: The agent causing Lyme disease had finally been found. In 1983, at the International Symposium of Lyme Disease, the Lyme bacterium was named *Borrelia burgdorferi* in honor of its discoverer.

CHAPTER TWO

Symptoms

In the past, Lyme disease was thought to be characterized by three stages, each of which had a list of worsening symptoms that were generally expected to occur if the illness was not halted by the person's immune system or discovered and treated by a doctor. These stages were known as early localized infection, early disseminated (spread out) infection, and late persistent (continuing) infection. In more recent years, however, experts have recognized that the disease does not always follow predictable time periods and the symptoms do not always follow each other in the same sequence. Due to this, the concept of Lyme having clear-cut, named stages has been dropped by many doctors and health organizations. Nonetheless, there are some symptoms typically experienced more often by people in the early period after being infected and some more often associated with the disease after it has been untreated for months or years. Many different parts of the body can be affected by Lyme, and not all patients experience the same symptoms—facts that can make diagnosis difficult for doctors unfamiliar with the disease.

Typical Symptoms of Early Infection

After a bite from a tick carrying *B. burgdorferi* sensu lato, Lyme infection starts in the skin and bloodstream. The most well-known symptom of Lyme disease—a red rash known as erythema migrans (EM)—usually appears anywhere from three to thirty days after the tick bite. (A rash that occurs immediately after a tick bite is most likely just an allergic reaction to the tick's saliva.) EM begins as a small, red area that expands over the next several days, sometimes becoming over 1 foot (30.48cm) in diameter if untreated, but often fading on its own after three to four weeks. This red inflammation is the result of the immune system beginning to fight against the foreign bacteria that have been introduced into the body.

As the spirochetes move away from the site of the bite, the immune reaction and inflammation follow, which in some cases cause the inner area of the rash to become paler in appearance and develop one or more bright red rings around it, giving it the appearance of a bull's-eye. This does not always occur, however, and in some people the rash is not circular in shape at all, but triangular, rectangular, or oval. EM is generally not painful, itchy, or scaly, but it can feel warm to the touch. The most common locations on the body for an EM rash are the armpits, waistline, groin, thighs, trunk, and the backs

The most well-known symptom of Lyme disease is a red rash known as erythema migrans that appears anywhere from three to thirty days after being bitten by a tick.

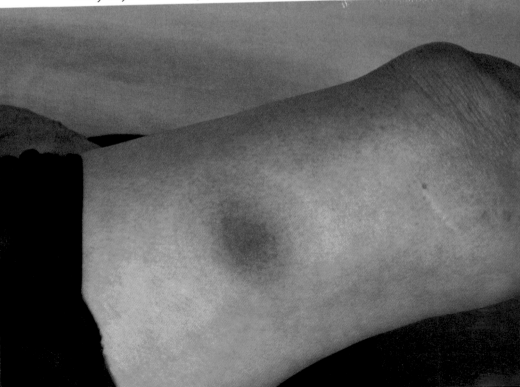

of the knees. As some of these areas are ones that are hard to see or that people do not often check, EM can sometimes go undetected.

As with many aspects of Lyme disease, there is disagreement in the medical profession over how many patients with Lyme will have the EM rash. According to the CDC, the figure is 80 percent, but according to the International Lyme and

As the immune system reacts and inflammation progresses, the EM rash can take on the appearance of a bull's-eye of a target.

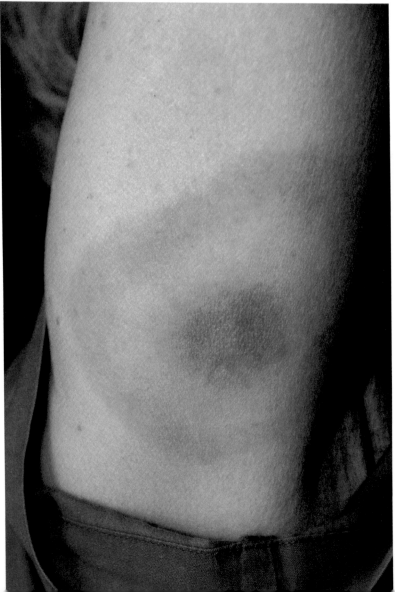

Associated Diseases Society, a nonprofit group of physicians dedicated to the diagnosis and treatment of Lyme disease, less than 50 percent of patients with Lyme recall having a rash. Regardless of where the truth lies, EM is so strongly associated with Lyme that, according to the Infectious Diseases Society of America, it is "the only manifestation of Lyme disease in the United States that is sufficiently distinctive enough to allow clinical diagnosis in the absence of laboratory confirmation."[4] In other words, if a doctor observes the EM rash on a patient, no further testing is necessary to prove that patient has Lyme disease.

Other symptoms often experienced by people not long after being bitten can include headaches, aches, a slight fever, chills, malaise (a general feeling of bodily discomfort), and fatigue. One Lyme sufferer named Bob describes his experience with the illness in its early days. "My body was achy beyond what I would expect from the physical activities I had been involved in," he recalls. "My body ached from my ankles to neck and included both my muscles and joints. Later that evening a dull headache and fever and chills came on. A few times I experienced what I describe as my head buzzing. At the time I thought I had food poisoning."[5]

The Disease Spreads

If a person infected with Lyme disease does not seek treatment, or if the immune system does not succeed in killing the spirochetes, the disease moves from the bloodstream to organs such as the heart, brain, and joints. When this occurs, the symptoms are varied and affect many areas of the body. They can include two or more EM rashes that are located at different spots than where the initial tick bite occurred, headaches, a stiff neck, tingling or numbness in the arms and legs, blurred vision, a high fever, severe fatigue, multiple enlarged lymph glands, a sore throat, a slowing of the heart, pains in the joints and muscles, and facial paralysis.

The facial paralysis that sometimes occurs with Lyme disease is similar to a condition known as Bell's palsy. The inflammation that comes with Lyme infection damages the nerves that control muscles on one side of the face, causing it to droop.

The person will have a lopsided smile and may drool and/or be unable to close the eye on the affected side of the face completely. They may also have pain in or around the ear, lose the ability to taste, or suffer from an increased sensitivity to sound. The paralysis is usually temporary and begins to improve within a few weeks.

Less likely to clear on their own, however, are the joint pains associated with Lyme as it moves through the body. These pains are most often associated with the larger joints such as the knees, elbows, or shoulders and can shift from one joint to another. The joints and tendons are not always visibly swollen at this point, and the pains come and go, with the infected person sometimes experiencing problems for a few days or weeks and then feeling fine for a period of time before the pain returns. As Bob's Lyme disease progressed, he began to experience these aches. He states, "I also wasn't able to walk normally due to the muscle and joint pain. I wasn't hobbled, but anyone looking at me would think I had a problem."[6]

Another Lyme sufferer who experienced advanced symptoms was Jason Weintraub, son of science journalist Pamela Weintraub, who also contracted Lyme along with her entire family. Pamela described her son's struggle with the infection in her 2008 book, *Cure Unknown: Inside the Lyme Epidemic*:

> Slowly the "flu" went away, but Jason never got well. He now had pain that traveled around his body from joint to joint, constant headache and stomachache, a hacking cough, and inexplicable [unexplained] insomnia and fatigue. His neck hurt so much that sometimes he could not lift his head from his pillow for days. He dropped from all his sports activities—they were simply too exhausting for him. He stopped doing his homework. He refused to see friends, even his two best friends. On more and more days he could not get up for school.[7]

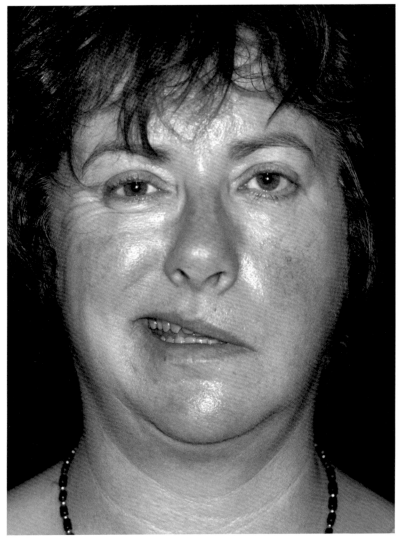

Bell's palsy is similar to a condition caused by Lyme disease, which results in damage to the nerves in the face that causes one side of the face to droop.

Neurological Lyme

Disorders of the brain and spinal cord can also occur with Lyme disease. If the Lyme spirochetes reach the central nervous system, it can cause a host of issues, including depression, hallucinations, panic attacks, seizures, memory problems, and paranoia.

Lyme in Europe

Lyme disease in Europe is typically caused by two strains of *B. burgdorferi* bacteria named *B. afzelii* and *B. garinii*, although some cases are caused by the primary U.S. strain, *B. burgdorferi* sensu stricto. The process of diagnosis and treatment for European Lyme disease is generally the same as in the United States.

Differences, however, can exist in the symptoms. While most are the same on both continents, European patients can also suffer from borrelial lymphocytoma, which is a bluish-reddish discoloration of the skin that usually occurs on the earlobe, breast, or scrotum. It is usually, though not always, caused by infection with *B. afzelii*. A second symptom found only in Europe—also affecting the skin and most frequently due to *B. afzelii* infection—is acrodermatitis chronica atrophicans. This condition is a chronic inflammation of the skin, usually on the arms or legs, which, if untreated, can lead to the skin atrophying (wasting away).

These are known as neurological symptoms, as *neurological* means "having to do with the nervous system." Hilary McDonald, at a 1996 Lyme disease rally in Washington, D.C., recounted her father's experience with the neurological symptoms of Lyme:

> My father was admitted to a local Savannah [Georgia] hospital because he was increasingly disoriented [confused] and my mother found it too difficult to care for him at home. He became very agitated, could not sleep, and paced the halls. He would not keep his clothes on, and his speech became difficult to understand. He was so disruptive to the other patients on his floor that he was moved to the "psyche unit." There he was straightjacketed and given drugs to "calm him down."[8]

One symptom often reported by Lyme sufferers with neurological involvement is what they sometimes refer to as "brain fog," which is characterized by lapses in memory, extreme fatigue, difficulty sleeping, and an inability to concentrate. Chris Le Hérou of Belgium, speaking during his ordeal, said:

> I do not see the world the same as before. I do not even know any more, when my car is stopped by a traffic light, if the light is red or green. I see only some of the vehicles I cross, or maybe I see them all, but my brain doesn't tell me anymore. I look like a lost puppy. I touch madness, and I have the impression that I shall find a refuge there. And I do not have energy any more. I want to sleep, sleep, as everything hurts me.[9]

Some Lyme sufferers experience extreme pain and sensitivity in their legs.

People with brain fog must sometimes search for words or names that would normally come easily to them or have difficulty with simple motor skills such as tying their shoes. In some cases, spatial memory is affected. Spatial memory is responsible for recording information about a person's environment and the placement of things within it. A Lyme patient displaying this symptom may go out to run an errand and find him- or herself unable to remember the route home afterward. According to psychiatrist Robert Bransfield, "One patient had a panic attack when they were lost in their garage and had lost the spatial awareness of the location of the door."[10]

Loss of sensation in the arms and legs, or a feeling of "pins and needles," also often occurs in this stage. Neurologist John Halperin discovered this was due to damage done to the body's nerve cells by the disease. In some Lyme sufferers, however, depending on which and how many cells are damaged, an opposite effect can result, and instead of numbness the person will complain of extreme pain and sensitivity, often in the legs. One stricken woman recalls:

> My legs had become so painful I could no longer stand in the shower; my ankles and the long bones in my calves and shins throbbed with pain—not an ache, but a feeling that someone had scraped the skin away, thrown salt into the raw tissue, then set it on fire! The "fat" part in the back of the calves was virtually untouchable. In despair, I resigned my job prematurely; though my supervisor had done everything humanly possible to accommodate me, I was dazed with this physical assault, and falling to pieces. I dragged myself to bed, rubbing liniment on my legs and holding ice to my mouth, and woke up angry in the night that I hadn't just died. Even the thinness of a sheet was too painful for my legs. At times, my feet felt burning hot, as though I'd stepped barefoot in fresh tar. Often, my legs would "pulsate"—as if someone were snapping their fingers all over, stinging, from the inside out.[11]

In rare cases, symptoms of late-stage Lyme can resemble those of a stroke, including severe weakness on one side of the body. The same woman who experienced the intense leg pains also notes: "I . . . couldn't use my right arm and hand at all—without the sling, the limb just hung limply by my side. I had no strength or motor control in my hand; I could not even grip a pencil, much less write. My arm was too weak to hold up a thin piece of paper."[12]

Other Advanced Symptoms

Approximately 60 percent of persons with Lyme that goes untreated for long periods will develop swelling and pain of one or more of the joints, which is sometimes referred to as Lyme arthritis. This typically involves one of the knees, but both

Lyme Throughout Time

Although Lyme is considered to have been discovered in the United States in the 1970s, the disease had been previously described by doctors in Europe for almost a century. In 1883, a German physician named Alfred Buchwald observed the first reported case of acrodermatitis chronica atrophicans, a progressive skin disorder associated with the European strains of Lyme disease.

In 1909 Swedish doctor Arvid Afzelius presented research he had done on an expanding skin rash that would later come to be known as erythema migrans (EM), the most well-known symptom of Lyme disease. In 1921, Afzelius made the connection between joint problems and the disease causing the rash. He also put forth the theory that the illness was transmitted by ticks. Further research by European doctors also associated neurologic symptoms with the disease.

Rudolph Scrimenti, a dermatologist (skin doctor), first documented the EM rash in the United States in 1970, five years before Lyme's official "discovery" in Connecticut by Allen Steere. Scrimenti successfully cured the patient with penicillin, basing his actions on those of European doctors who had treated the disease.

large and small joints can be affected, including those of the hands. In some cases, the joint where the lower jaw connects to the skull is painful. The pain attacks are often intermittent (come and go) and usually involve only one or two joints at a time.

Another less common but serious complication of Lyme is involvement of the heart. Four to 10 percent of Lyme patients develop heart problems. These can include conduction defects (problems with the electrical pathways and muscle fibers that conduct impulses through the heart), an unusually rapid heart rate accompanied by an irregular rhythm, or inflammation of the heart wall and the sac surrounding it.

Finally, Lyme can also affect a person's eyesight. Symptoms in this category can range from irritating—a sensitivity to light and the appearance of "floaters"—to very critical if inflammation of the optic nerve or the brain due to the spirochete invasion results in vision loss. The cornea or middle layer of the eye may also become inflamed, both of which can also lead to loss of vision.

Symptoms Can Mislead or Confuse

Diagnosing Lyme disease from symptoms alone can be difficult. Unless a person remembers being bitten by a tick or displays the telltale EM rash, a doctor will probably not immediately suspect Lyme, especially if the area in which the sick person lives is not considered a hot spot for the disease. Many doctors in nonendemic locations are simply not very familiar with Lyme and may not recognize it even with the proper clues in place. In the Lyme documentary *Under Our Skin*, Jordan Fisher Smith of Nevada City, California, recalls his difficulty in obtaining a correct diagnosis:

> My case was sort of cut and dried. A) I was a park ranger. B) I knew exactly when I was bitten and I saved the tick and brought it to my doctor. C) I had a red rash. And D) I had a rather classic case of neurological Lyme with all the usual trimmings. But I brought all that to the doctors and it took five doctors to figure it out.[13]

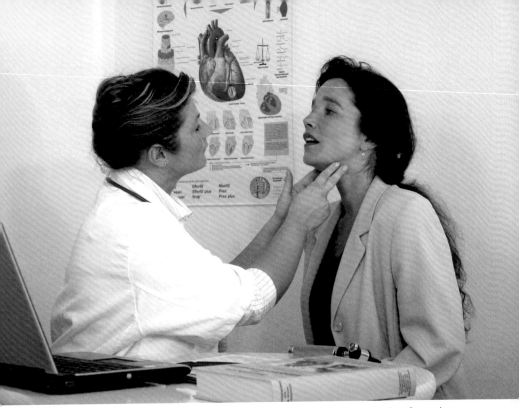

One difficulty in diagnosing Lyme disease is due to the fact that its early symptoms are similar to those of the flu.

Smith estimates his illness, which he says probably could have been cured with a single bottle of antibiotics if correctly diagnosed in its early days, wound up costing him seventy-five thousand to one hundred thousand dollars in doctor visits and incorrect medications.

Another difficulty faced by doctors and patients is that the symptoms of Lyme can often resemble those of other illnesses. Lyme in the early stage of infection, if no rash is present, can easily be mistaken for the flu. Lyme symptoms of fatigue, sore throat, fever, swollen lymph nodes, and skin rash can mimic those of the viral infection known as mononucleosis, or the "kissing disease." If Lyme progresses to the early neurological stage, the headache, stiff neck, and fatigue resemble the symptoms of viral meningitis, an inflammation of the membranes that surround the brain and spinal cord. In children, the joint pains associated with Lyme can be misdiagnosed as juvenile rheumatoid arthritis, as happened in Lyme, Connecticut, before Allen Steere's investigation began. Other tick-borne illnesses, such as tick-borne relapsing fever and Rocky Mountain spotted fever, also share many symptoms in common with Lyme disease.

The symptoms of Lyme can be frustrating both in how nonspecific or misleading they can sometimes be and also in their on-again, off-again nature. Infected persons may believe that they are getting better when symptoms disappear, thus deciding against seeking medical treatment, only to start feeling ill again a few weeks later. Sufferers can have spotty attendance at work or school, and the explanation of what exactly is wrong is not always easy to give without a correct diagnosis. Brian Fallon, director of the Lyme and Tick-Borne Disease Research Center at New York's Columbia University, states: "I think there are a number of general aspects of Lyme disease that cause distress and confusion. One is that symptoms fluctuate. Patients often feel worse on some days, better on others. That confuses parents, school systems, employers, spouses. It's a difficult aspect of this illness."[14]

Coinfections

Another issue that can complicate almost every aspect of Lyme disease, from symptoms to diagnosis to treatment, is that of coinfections. Lyme is not the only disease that can be transmitted by ticks, and if a person is bitten by a tick carrying *B. burgdorferi* sensu lato *and* bacteria that causes one of these other illnesses, the person can have a coinfection.

Two of the most common diseases found in these coinfections are babesiosis and ehrlichiosis. Babesiosis is caused by a parasite called *Babesia microti*, which destroys a person's red blood cells. (A parasite is an organism that lives in or on another organism from which it feeds.) Ehrlichiosis, like Lyme, is transmitted by a bacterium. Two types of ehrlichiosis have been identified in the United States: human monocytic ehrlichiosis, which is caused by bacteria called *Ehrlichia chaffeensis*, and human granulocytic ehrlichiosis, which is caused by *Anaplasma phagocytophilum*. The terms *monocyte* and *granulocyte* in the names of the diseases refer to the types of white blood cells in the body that are attacked by the bacteria.

If a person has a coinfection, the difficulties he can face can begin early, with the onset of symptoms. A doctor who might otherwise suspect Lyme disease may be misdirected because the coinfection is causing additional symptoms that are not typical of Lyme. Many of the symptoms of Lyme, babesiosis, and ehrlichiosis, however, *are* the same—fever, aches, fatigue—which can also confuse a physician trying to make a diagnosis. Symptoms can also be worse and/or last longer in persons with coinfections. According to one study, patients infected with both Lyme and babesiosis had an average of three more symptoms and were sicker an average of two weeks longer than persons infected with Lyme only.

Although babesiosis, human granulocytic ehrlichiosis, and human monocytic ehrlichiosis are the best-known of the possible Lyme coinfections, they could be merely the tip of the iceberg. Other disease-causing microbes (tiny life-forms) carried by ticks are being researched by scientists worldwide, and further findings seem likely. As science journalist and Lyme sufferer Pamela Weintraub states, "Alone and in combination, microbes transmitted by ticks can make us ill, and for each known infection, another tick-borne pathogen may be awaiting discovery in the wings. As long as we live in suburbs abutting the woods we'll be in the path of the tick tornado and its toxic output."[15]

CHAPTER THREE

Diagnosis and Treatment

To diagnose Lyme disease, the Centers for Disease Control and Prevention (CDC) recommends that doctors consider the patient's symptoms and whether or not the patient's history shows a probable exposure to infected ticks. Serological tests—tests that examine blood serum—are also helpful in making a diagnosis. (Blood serum is the amber-colored clear liquid that separates from blood when it is allowed to clot.) It is extremely difficult, time-consuming, and expensive to locate actual spirochetes in bodily fluids or organs, so the serological tests for Lyme that are usually performed are what are known as indirect tests. This means that instead of measuring the presence of the bacteria itself, the tests measure the body's reaction to the bacteria's presence. This is done by measuring the antibodies produced to fight the infection. Antibodies are specialized proteins generated by white blood cells that recognize and target organisms that invade the body—in this case, the *Borrelia* bacteria—and seek to kill them. Any invading organism that causes antibodies to be produced is known as an antigen.

To test for Lyme antibodies, doctors currently use a two-step method consisting of a screening test known as an ELISA and a more specific confirmatory test known as a Western blot. These tests, however, can be problematic and are not without their critics among both patients and medical professionals.

ELISA

ELISA stands for enzyme-linked immunosorbent assay. In this test, a person's blood serum is diluted (thinned out) with water and, along with one undiluted sample, placed into a plastic tray with numerous wells in it. In each well is a tiny amount of dead Lyme bacteria. If antibodies to the bacteria exist in the blood serum, they will stick to the bottom of the well and will remain after the wells are rinsed with purified water. If no antibodies are present, the serum is completely washed away.

Next, another solution is added to the wells. This solution contains antibodies that react to other antibodies. These second antibodies have an enzyme linked to them. An enzyme is a protein that can produce certain chemical changes in organic substances. In the case of the ELISA, this enzyme causes dye to change colors.

After the second antibodies and the linked enzyme have been added to the wells, the plastic tray is incubated for an

A microbiologist performs an ELISA test by diluting a patient's blood and analyzing it.

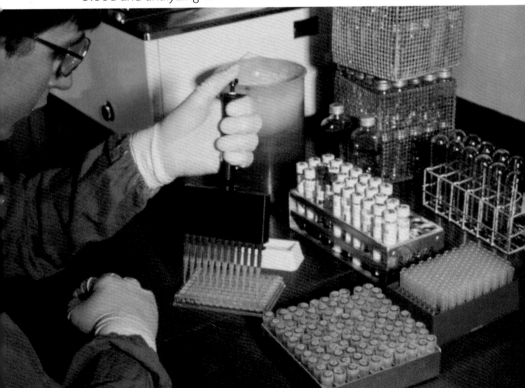

hour and rinsed out again. If antibodies to the Lyme bacteria were present, the second antibodies will have detected and bound to them and they will still be stuck in the wells. The dye is then added to the wells, and if the second antibodies are still present, the dye will change color. The greater the color change, the more antibodies that were found. This—the presence of antibodies to Lyme in the blood serum—indicates the person being tested has been exposed to the disease.

A similar test called an indirect fluorescent antibody is sometimes used instead of an ELISA, but it is considered less accurate and is generally only performed if an ELISA is not available.

Western Blot

If a person's ELISA comes back positive or if the results are unclear, a Western blot test is then performed. This more precise test allows the laboratory or hospital to determine exactly which antigens the person's blood serum has developed antibodies against. This is particularly useful since other antigens similar to those responsible for Lyme (such as the pathogens that cause syphilis, mononucleosis, and AIDS) can also bind with the antibodies produced against Lyme. This is known as cross-reacting.

In a Western blot, *B. burgdorferi* bacteria are put into a detergent that breaks up the proteins from which it is made. These proteins have different sizes and are electrically charged. The proteins are placed onto a gel that contains many holes and spaces, and an electrical current is applied to the gel. This causes the proteins to move through the nooks and crannies of the gel, with the smaller proteins moving the fastest and reaching the bottom of the gel first. Once the proteins have all been grouped according to size, they are blotted from the gel substance onto a nylon membrane and separated into bands. When a person's blood serum is introduced to the proteins on the membrane, if antibodies to any of the proteins are present in the serum, those antibodies will bind to that specific protein band. A dye is attached to the serum that will cause a

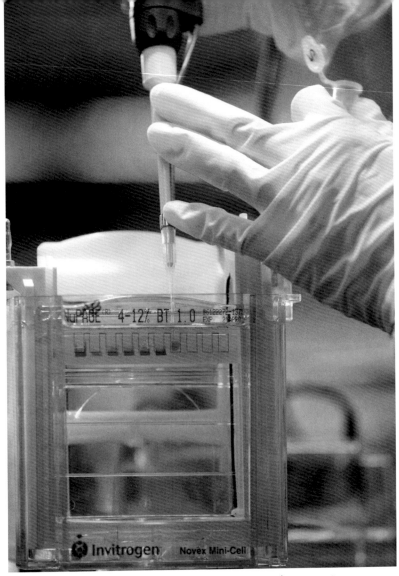

A lab technician performs a Western blot test by inserting samples of *B. burgdorferi* bacteria into wells filled with detergent that will break up the proteins the bacteria are made of.

band with antibodies attached to it to turn a color for easier identification.

The current CDC standard for a Western blot to be positive states that for early stage infection, two of three specific protein bands must be "lit," or have antibodies attach to them so the dye causes the color change. For a person in the latter stages of the disease to be considered positive, five of ten bands must be lit.

Are These Tests Effective?

Many experts agree that the ELISA and Western blot tests, despite being the diagnostic standard for Lyme, are by no means perfect. One basic shortcoming of the ELISA test is that it is not always effective in the very early stage of Lyme infection. If a person is given an ELISA test before the body has had a chance to produce antibodies to the bacteria—a process that can take days or weeks—the ELISA will be negative, even though that person may indeed have Lyme disease. This is especially critical in patients who do not have the telltale EM rash. If a doctor does not observe a rash and an ELISA test is negative, a case of Lyme that could have been caught early and treated promptly may be missed. In addition, the test does not recognize the difference between a present, active infection and a past one. In some cases, antibodies can linger in the body for years, so if someone was infected with Lyme in the past but recovered, he or she can still have a positive test.

Another problem is that all ELISA and Western blot tests are not evaluated at the same place. Many different laboratories and hospitals perform the tests, and the degree of accuracy can vary. In an experiment conducted by doctors in the mid-1980s, samples of a patient's blood serum were sent to two separate labs. The serum tested positive for Lyme disease at one and negative at the other. Then the doctors sent samples of a single patient's blood serum to labs but labeled the samples as though they were from more than one person. In some cases, the samples were reported as testing positive, while other samples, from the exact same patient and being evaluated at the exact same lab, were reported as testing negative. Interpreting, or "reading," the tests is not always a straightforward issue. Paul Fawcett, a specialist in Lyme blood tests, speaks of the difficulties in interpreting a Western blot:

> Some of these bands lie within a millimeter [of each other]. You can't be sure that a band you're calling positive is really the correct one. Look at the CAP [College of American Pathologists] surveys . . . different labs using the same samples and the same strips are getting different

results, showing different bands. The manufactured kits contain a . . . test strip that's used [to determine which bands are which]. You can line up the test strip and the strip from the patient and you have to slide them back and forth to properly line them up.[16]

How the CDC Classifies Cases of Lyme

The Centers for Disease Control and Prevention (CDC) records all cases of Lyme disease that are reported by doctors across the country. There are three classifications that a reported case can be given—confirmed, probable, or suspected—depending on whether or not it meets certain guidelines:

Confirmed: a case of EM with a known exposure, a case of EM with laboratory evidence of infection and without a known exposure, or a case with at least one late manifestation that has laboratory evidence of infection.

Probable: any other case of physician-diagnosed Lyme disease that has laboratory evidence of infection.

Suspected: a case of EM where there is no known exposure and no laboratory evidence of infection, or a case with laboratory evidence of infection but no clinical information available (such as a laboratory report).

For the purpose of these guidelines, "known exposure" means that the patient had been in an area where Lyme disease is endemic for thirty days or less before the EM rash appeared. The necessary "laboratory evidence of infection" would be either spirochetes discovered directly from a skin culture or positive results from serological tests for Lyme antibodies. The CDC notes that if the only symptom is "tick bite" or "insect bite," the illness will not be considered to be Lyme.

More controversial are arguments that the tests themselves are flawed because of how they were originally created or because of what information is considered important or not when they are evaluated. Critics point out that the band pattern approved by the CDC for a Western blot result to be considered positive was decided upon using a single strain of *B. burgdorferi*, when there are hundreds of strains of the bacteria worldwide, each with protein coats that can vary and thus cause different antibody-binding patterns, or different bands to be lit.

A researcher analyzes a Western blot test. The tests are difficult to interpret because the bands are within a millimeter of each other and not easy to discern.

A second major complaint made by some doctors and Lyme patients has to do with two protein bands that the scientists who conceived the Western blot decided to leave off the test. These two proteins, outer surface protein A and outer surface protein B, are "both so specific to the Lyme spirochete that they could come from nothing but exposure to *B. burgdorferi* and were even candidates for making Lyme vaccines,"[17] according to science journalist Pamela Weintraub. The reason given for not including these two protein bands was that they were not among the ten most common bands that Lyme patients lit. According to Lyme pioneer Allen Steere, if those two bands were going to show up, the other, more common bands would as well, so it was not statistically necessary to include OspA and OspB.

Coinfections can also affect the serological tests used to diagnose Lyme. According to physician Jonathan A. Edlow, scientists at New York's Westchester County Medical Center found that in patients confirmed to be infected only with human granulocytic ehrlichiosis, most of them also tested positive for Lyme, even though they did not have Lyme.

Despite these shortcomings, the CDC maintains the two-step ELISA and Western blot method is highly effective in diagnosing Lyme. Experts claim that in latter phases of the disease, the ELISA test is about 95 percent sensitive and 95 percent specific. This means that it will give a positive result in 95 percent of people who truly have the disease and a negative result in 95 percent of those who truly do not. Not surprisingly, these statistics are disputed by other experts and patient advocates, who claim the numbers are actually much lower. Scientists at Stony Brook University Medical Center, who have done large amounts of research on Lyme, have suggested that a better way to diagnose the illness might be to run the tests on a patient several times over an extended period of time to look for changes in the results. This is rarely done, however.

Direct Tests

Although these indirect, serological tests are most frequently used to diagnose Lyme, there are others administered far less often that seek to detect the actual DNA of the *B. burgdorferi* bacteria rather than just antibodies formed against it. These are known as direct tests.

In the early stage of Lyme, if an EM rash is present, the doctor can do a skin culture. A sample of the infected skin is taken and sent to a laboratory, where it is tested for the presence of the bacteria. This is done by placing the sample in a container called a petri dish. The dish is full of nutrients that encourage any bacteria present in the sample to grow so they can be observed under a microscope. Although this method is highly reliable, it can be very time consuming, as it generally takes several weeks to get the results. During this time, the infection—if it is indeed Lyme—can spread further into the body and the patient's health can worsen. Additionally, if an EM rash is present, it is often unnecessary to do a skin culture since the EM rash itself is considered enough evidence to confirm a diagnosis of Lyme.

One direct test that was recently developed is the Lyme Dot Blot Assay, which searches for the presence of B. *burgdorferi* in a person's urine. In this process, the urine is processed to isolate the antigens in it, which are then bound to a membrane and incubated with antibodies to B. *burgdorferi*. Then, as with the ELISA test, a second antibody is used to detect the presence of antibodies to the Lyme bacteria. A color-developing solution is then applied to the membrane, and dots on the membrane containing antigens that are reacting to the antibodies will turn blue. If the Lyme Dot Blot Assay comes up positive, the results are often confirmed using what is known as a reverse Western blot. Whereas the regular Western blot detects the presence of antibodies to the Lyme bacteria, the reverse Western blot detects the presence of the bacteria themselves.

Another test used is the polymerase chain reaction (PCR) test. Typically, a PCR test is performed using either spinal fluid or fluid collected with a hollow needle from an affected joint. If spirochetes are present in the sample, the PCR takes part of the DNA of the bacteria and uses an enzyme to make millions of copies of it, so it is easy to detect using a microscope. A PCR test is rarely performed, because it requires technical

A technician places samples in a Cobas Amplicor machine as part of a PCR test of a sample of bacterial DNA and uses an enzyme to make millions of copies of it.

skill beyond that required in a laboratory setting and is very expensive. Another stumbling block is that *B. burgdorferi* bacteria do not tend to remain in these fluids for long, instead preferring to attach to nerve and joint tissues. Finally, a PCR test is a delicate process, and the fluid sample can be easily contaminated by other DNA molecules that may be floating around the lab. This can cause what is known as a false positive result, which is a result that says a person has a disease when in fact he or she does not.

Antibiotic Treatments

If it is determined that a person is in fact suffering from Lyme disease, he or she is given antibiotics, which are drugs used to treat infections caused by bacteria. For adults who appear to be in the early stage of the infection—for example, who have an EM rash and flu-like symptoms but do not seem to be having any neurological issues—the guidelines set down by the Infectious Diseases Society of America (IDSA) suggest a two- to three-week course (series of doses) of antibiotics. The specific antibiotics they recommend are doxycycline, amoxicillin, or cefuroxime axetil, given orally, which means in a form that can be swallowed, such as a pill or capsule. For children under eight years of age, amoxicillin or cefuroxime axetil can be prescribed, but not doxycycline, as it can cause a permanent yellowing or graying of the teeth and/or affect the child's growth. Likewise, women who are pregnant or breast-feeding should not take doxycycline as it can affect the baby's bone and tooth development.

Patients with Lyme that suffer from neurological symptoms may require antibiotics that are given intravenously. This is when a needle is inserted into the person's vein and the medicine, in a liquid form, is pushed through the needle and directly into the bloodstream. Adults are usually given either ceftriaxone (also known as Rocephin) or penicillin, while children are prescribed either ceftriaxone or cefotaxime.

Lyme patients with neurological symptoms may be given antibiotics intravenously.

A person with heart problems thought to be caused by early Lyme is usually treated with either oral or intravenous antibiotics for two weeks. In some cases, they may need to be hospitalized and constantly monitored due to the high risk of life-threatening complications. Patients with advanced heart block (a problem with the heart's electrical system that controls the rate and rhythm of heartbeats) may need to be placed on a pacemaker, which is a small machine placed under the skin on the chest that helps the heart maintain a more normal rhythm. The pacemaker is removed when the heart problem is cured.

In adults and children over eight, Lyme arthritis that is not accompanied by any neurological symptoms is typically treated with doxycycline, amoxicillin, or cefuroxime axetil given orally for four weeks. If the joint pain and swelling improve but do not completely clear, another four-week course of oral antibiotics is prescribed. If these symptoms do not improve at all or worsen, intravenous antibiotics (ceftriaxone, penicillin, or cefotaxime) are recommended. If the nervous system is also involved, however, the IDSA guidelines suggest the patient be treated with intravenous antibiotics immediately rather than taking an oral course first.

One change made to the IDSA guidelines in the past few years is the addition of a treatment recommendation for a person who has recently been bitten by a tick but has not shown any symptoms of Lyme. The person must be considered at a high risk for contracting the disease from the bite, and the incident must meet three standards: (1) the tick must be reliably identified as an *Ixodes scapularis* tick, and it must have been attached to the person for at least thirty-six hours; (2) the treatment must be able to be started within seventy-two hours after the tick is removed; and (3) the person must live in an area in which the tick population has a high rate of Lyme infection. If all these standards are met, the person may be prescribed a single dose of doxycycline.

Coinfections can complicate treatment. Some of the antibiotics recommended to treat Lyme have no or little effect on other

Jarisch-Herxheimer Reaction

One complication of Lyme disease treatment sometimes reported by patients is what is known as the Jarisch-Herxheimer reaction. Commonly referred to as a "herx," this reaction occurs when the antibiotics target and kill the invading bacteria. As they die, the bacteria can release toxins into the body that can make a person actually feel temporarily more sick, even though their illness is in the process of being cured. Symptoms generally include fever, chills, joint and/or muscle pain, and headache. This reaction can be frightening to patients who are expecting to feel better, not worse.

Virginia Scherr, a psychiatrist and Lyme sufferer, recalls her experience with a Jarisch-Herxheimer reaction:

> At first, things rapidly got worse. A sense of urgency, fear, and uncertainty tinged everything. Several times I reached out to other physicians by phone at night because I could no longer tell whether what was happening to me was important or was trivial. Routine noises elicited startled reactions. I had a nurse stay with me when I was alone because I was so unsure of what was happening neurologically. I later learned this flurry of symptoms was a Jarisch-Herxheimer reaction to the kill-off of the spirochetes.

Virginia Scherr. "The Physician as a Patient: Lyme Disease, Ehrlichiosis, and Babesiosis—a Recounting of a Personal Experience with Tick-Borne Diseases." International Lyme and Associated Diseases Society, January 2000. www.ilads.org/lyme_research/lyme_publications22.html.

illnesses such as babesiosis and ehrlichiosis. For example, ehrlichiosis can be treated with doxycycline, like Lyme, but whereas Lyme can also be treated with amoxicillin or cefuroxime, these antibiotics do not work as well in curing ehrlichiosis. Thus, unless the doctor knows or suspects a coinfection, in some cases it can seem as though a Lyme patient is not responding to the recommended medication. Edlow describes the problem:

> Should coinfection affect how treatment failures for Lyme are viewed? Should they affect how the manifestations of Lyme disease are defined? Imagine a patient who was bitten by a tick that happened to be infected with the agent of [human granulocytic ehrlichiosis] and *B. burgdorferi*. . . . Suppose the patient is treated with amoxicillin—a perfectly appropriate antibiotic choice for Lyme disease—but he or she does not respond to it. Is this a treatment failure of amoxicillin in Lyme disease? If the physician knew that the patient had a coinfection, the answer to these questions would be relatively simple, but if the physician did not know of the coinfection, he or she might draw incorrect conclusions.[18]

According to the CDC, persons in the early stages of Lyme who are treated with antibiotics typically have rapid and complete recoveries. Patients with Lyme that was left undiagnosed and untreated for longer periods may not be so lucky. While late Lyme can usually be treated effectively, the process can take longer and require more than one course of antibiotic therapy. Additionally, even after the infection has been cleared by the antibiotics, symptoms may be slow to vanish.

Alternative Therapies

Some patients who continue to experience symptoms after being treated for Lyme disease do not want to seek further medical treatment—or are unable to due to a lack of money or access to a doctor they feel can correctly address the illness. These patients sometimes turn to alternative treatments in an effort to feel better. Alternative treatments generally do not have clinical studies accepted by the medical establishment that support their effectiveness, and some are even considered dangerous. These treatments can range from fairly simple, such as taking mineral supplements, to more complex.

One of the more involved treatments is called the Marshall Protocol. The creator of the protocol believes that pathogens such as Lyme bacteria block the body's vitamin D receptor, which plays an important role in the body's immune reaction. His theory states the pathogens keep the vitamin D receptor from producing the agents that would normally kill the pathogens, thus allowing them the freedom to spread throughout the body's cells. In the protocol, patients take olmesartan (which improves blood flow), low doses of antibiotics, and avoid certain kinds of vitamin D supplements and sunlight.

Other people have claimed they benefited from treatments in a hyperbaric oxygen chamber. In these sessions, a person sits or lies in the chamber for thirty to ninety minutes and is exposed to air that is 100 percent pure oxygen at higher than normal atmospheric pressure. This increases blood flow throughout the body and is believed to enhance the performance of the immune system.

Another alternative treatment is a salt/vitamin C protocol, in which a person ingests eight to sixteen grams of unprocessed salt (not the standard kind sold in stores) and eight to sixteen grams of vitamin C per day. The dosage of each starts low and increases as the treatment progresses. According to Bryan Rosner, author of *The Top 10 Lyme Disease Treatments*, this protocol is beneficial because salt enhances the effectiveness of a certain enzyme that contributes to white blood cell function and the immune system. He claims that vitamin C when used with salt speeds up the healing process and helps remove toxins from the body.

One of the stranger treatments people have turned to are rife machines. These machines supposedly work by directing an electromagnetic frequency through the body that breaks apart harmful pathogens. Different illnesses have different frequencies that the user programs into the machine. The frequency waves enter the body through electrodes (conductors) the person holds in both hands or that are attached to the feet or another part of the body.

Unfortunately, some out-of-the-ordinary treatments for Lyme disease have ended with tragic results. John Toth, a physician in Kansas, treated patients with injections of a com-

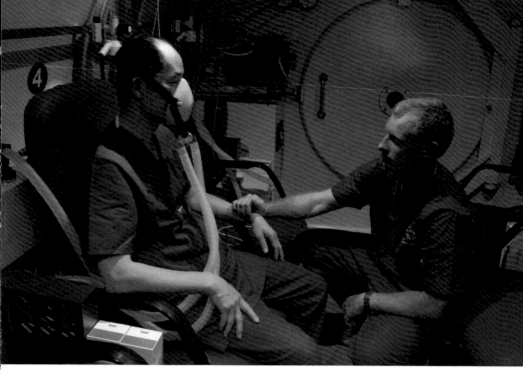

Some Lyme disease sufferers have claimed benefits from time spent in a hyperbaric oxygen chamber, which they believe enhances the immune system's performance.

pound called bismacine, which he and some other practitioners were promoting as a cure for Lyme disease. Bismacine had not been studied or proved effective for treating Lyme disease, and worse, it contains high amounts of the metal bismuth and can cause heart and kidney failure. One of Toth's patients, Beverly Wunder, fell into a coma and later died. Toth pleaded guilty to reckless involuntary manslaughter and spent time in prison. During his trial, Wunder's daughter stated her mother never even had Lyme disease, claiming "a doctor's greed and disregard for medical regulations and the value of human life cost my mother hers and has forever altered mine."[19] Eventually, the U.S. Food and Drug Administration (FDA) issued warnings to consumers that bismacine is not an approved drug to treat Lyme disease and is potentially fatal.

CHAPTER FOUR

The Aftermath of Infection

Despite receiving the recommended antibiotic treatment, 10 to 20 percent of people with Lyme disease do not seem to recover and instead continue to experience symptoms. Some of these patients, as well as a number of so-called Lyme-literate doctors who treat large numbers of Lyme cases—often with methods not recommended by the major medical organizations—claim this can mean the infection has not actually been cleared—a topic hotly debated in the Lyme community.

Chronic Lyme: Fact or Fiction?

Chronic Lyme has been defined as long-lasting or recurring symptoms that begin at the time a person becomes infected with *B. burgdorferi* sensu lato and continue for months or years, even after adequate antibiotics have been given. But does it actually exist?

A relatively small but vocal group of doctors and patients believe that it does. Many of these doctors are members of the International Lyme and Associated Diseases Society (ILADS). According to the ILADS website: "Many patients with chronic Lyme disease require prolonged treatment until the patient is symptom-free. Relapses occur and retreatment may be required. There are no tests currently available to prove that the organism is eradicated [wiped out] or that the patient with chronic Lyme disease is cured."[20] These doctors point to studies done on mice and dogs in which spirochetes were found in bodily fluids even after the proper course of antibiotic treatment had been followed. (These studies have not been performed using humans since humans cannot be sacrificed and autopsied like animals.)

Most doctors, however, including those responsible for creating the widely used Infectious Diseases Society of America (IDSA) guidelines for treating Lyme, do not believe in chronic Lyme. They contend that in most patients who claim to have it no evidence can be found of *B. burgdorferi* spirochetes still persisting in the body, and antibiotic treatment for longer than four weeks is not recommended.

Most of these physicians use the term "post-Lyme syndrome" rather than "chronic Lyme" and believe the likely cause of continued symptoms is an autoimmune disease triggered

A patient consults a doctor over treatment for chronic Lyme disease. No tests are available that can prove conclusively that the organism that causes the illness is able to be eradicated completely from a person's body.

by the Lyme infection. An autoimmune disease is one that occurs when a person's immune system mistakenly attacks and destroys healthy bodily tissue. Another theory states that the patients experiencing long-lasting symptoms never had Lyme in the first place, but rather have some other disease. If they were never infected with Lyme, it would make sense that they would not necessarily be cured by the accepted medications used to treat it.

If Not Lyme, Then What?

Another reason many doctors do not believe in chronic Lyme disease is that they suspect the symptoms can in fact point to another illness altogether. According to New York Medical College's Raymond Dattwyler, one of the doctors who created the IDSA treatment guidelines, "The majority of people who get the diagnosis of chronic Lyme disease have either depression, fibromyalgia, or another chronic disease. . . . The tragedy is that sometimes really serious, treatable diseases are ignored."[21]

Fibromyalgia is a condition that causes extended, body-wide pain and tenderness in joints, muscles, and tendons. It can also cause fatigue and sleep disorders. There is no known cause for fibromyalgia—occasionally it arises after a physical or emotional trauma or an illness, but often there appears to be no particular reason a person begins experiencing pain. There are no tests that can be used to confirm a diagnosis of fibromyalgia, and no drug that can cure it. Patients are generally told to take aspirin or acetaminophen for the pain and antidepressants to assist in sleeping. Physical therapy and counseling are also often recommended.

Another condition that doctors feel is often misdiagnosed as chronic Lyme disease is chronic fatigue syndrome (CFS). This disorder causes extreme fatigue that does not improve with rest or sleep and can worsen with physical or mental activity. Some of its other common symptoms resemble those of Lyme: loss of memory or concentration, a sore throat, enlarged lymph nodes, pain that moves from one joint to another, and headache. Like fibromyalgia, the cause of CFS is unknown,

Charles Ray Jones

Lyme-literate pediatrician Charles Ray Jones has treated thousands of children with Lyme disease. He graduated from New York Medical College in 1962 and went on to intern in pediatrics at New York City's St. Luke's Hospital. He then held the position of chief resident at New York's Memorial Sloan-Kettering Cancer Center, one of the top cancer hospitals in the nation, before going into private practice in Connecticut.

Jones is a firm believer in chronic Lyme disease and treats his patients with long-term antibiotic treatment. He estimates that about 80 percent of the cases he treats are children with chronic Lyme, and that of those cases, 75 percent are now completely recovered. According to him, by treating long term "you're enabling a child to be well and fulfill their genetic potential, in terms of going to school, being part of the workforce, and contributing to society's well-being."

Jones has the support of his patients and their parents. When the state's medical board brought charges against Jones, his supporters rallied to help pay his attorney's fees and attended his hearings before the board. One woman, who came from Florida, explained why: "You have to understand how important and beloved Jones is in the Lyme community. He's saved a lot of children. That's why people call him a saint. I'll do everything I can for this man."

Quoted in Gary Santaniello. "Lyme Disease Divide." *Hartford (CT) Courant*, September 17, 2006. http://articles.courant.com/2006-09-17/features/0609150349_1_lyme-disease-corkscrew-shaped-bacterium-lyme-bacterium.

and there are no laboratory tests for it or specific medication to treat it.

Depression is perhaps the most controversial disorder that doctors say can be mistaken for chronic Lyme disease. As with fibromyalgia and CFS, some of the symptoms of depression are the same as those experienced by Lyme sufferers, such as slowed thinking, decreased concentration, insomnia, fatigue,

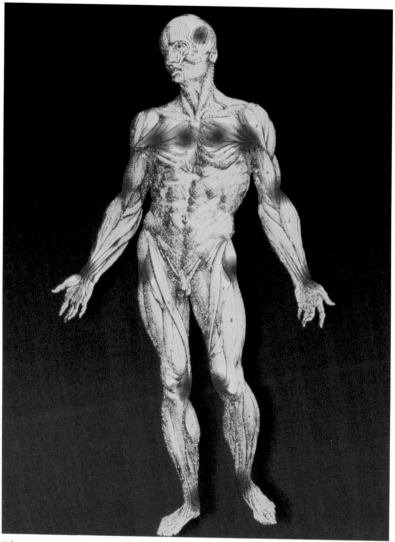

Fibromyalgia is a condition that causes body-wide pain and tenderness in joints and muscles (red areas). Lyme disease is sometimes misdiagnosed as fibromyalgia.

and unexplained body aches and pains. It can be very difficult for a patient to hear that a doctor thinks his or her problem is a mental, rather than a physical, one. "Mentally, I've been diagnosed with borderline personality, manic-depression (now called bipolar disorder), early morning depression, light-deprivation depression and just plain old depressed depression," says Jentri Anders. "I question how one distinguishes between depression and oppression."[22]

Eugene Shapiro of the Yale Medical Group says he understands why some people prefer a diagnosis of chronic Lyme to an alternative: "They'd rather have Lyme disease than multiple sclerosis, which has no cure. They'd rather have Lyme disease than depression, which carries a stigma [a sign of social unacceptability]. They'd rather have Lyme disease than something that nobody can figure out."[23]

The Case for Extended Treatment

Lyme-literate doctors take issue with this attitude, which they see as another attempt to deny the existence of chronic Lyme. Raphael Stricker, an ILADS officer, says of the patients whose concerns he feels are being dismissed: "The IDSA is basically saying to them, 'We're right, you're wrong, we don't want to listen to you, just take some antidepressants and go away.'"[24]

Doctors like Stricker are willing to treat patients they believe have chronic Lyme with antibiotics for much longer than is recommended by the IDSA guidelines, and they cite many instances of patients with persistent symptoms who experienced either an improvement or a complete recovery from these symptoms after such treatment. Marie Turley of Tennessee is one such patient. She was bitten by a tick in 1990 and developed symptoms of Lyme shortly after. She failed the laboratory tests for Lyme twice, however, finally receiving a positive Western blot on the third try, a year after the bite occurred. It was only after finding a doctor who agreed to give her prolonged antibiotic treatment for over three years that she felt she had recovered. In her words, "If I had not been fortunate enough . . . to locate a doctor courageous enough to treat me, I believe that I would either be dead now or crippled, bedridden, and severely mentally ill."[25]

The Lyme landscape is dotted with patients like Turley who credit doctors willing to ignore the IDSA guidelines. Kenneth Liegner, an ILADS member, says: "When I first started treating,

I treated by the book, but it became very clear those regimens weren't working. It was a gradual process from observing my patients that it began to dawn on me that the treatment we were giving wasn't treating the infection."[26]

These Lyme-literate doctors have several explanations as to why Lyme can be such a difficult disease to cure. Antibodies work by recognizing the outer protein of an antigen and binding to it. A Lyme bacterium, however, can change its outer protein coat, fooling the antibody into ignoring it. Also, after a person has been infected with Lyme for a longer period of time, the spirochetes move to areas of the body that do not receive much blood flow, which makes it difficult for antibiotics to reach them.

In addition, some scientists believe that spirochetes can evade antibodies *and* antibiotics by actually hiding inside other body cells. Another theory is that, if faced with unwelcome conditions, a spirochete can build a cyst around itself with a wall that cannot be penetrated by antibiotics. The spirochete can remain inside the cyst until conditions inside the body improve for it, then it will reemerge. In these cases, the antibiotics typically prescribed for Lyme would not be effective, and different medications would be needed to combat the bacteria. These two theories have only been proved when working with the spirochetes in a laboratory setting and have not yet been observed inside a living organism. However, some patients that have been treated on the strength of the theories have reported improvement. As Pamela Weintraub says about her own experience:

> Could Lyme form cysts? Just in case it did, I was treated with Flagyl. Could the spirochetes hide in cells? Whether or not they did, Biaxin combined with Plaquenil penetrated the body's cells and also worked for Lyme disease; for whatever reason, that drug cocktail alone relieved the infernal buzzing and tingling all over my body, detaching me finally from the neurological power grid of Lyme. . . . No matter what I did, when I stopped medicine altogether, a grinding fatigue and malaise always eventually returned.[27]

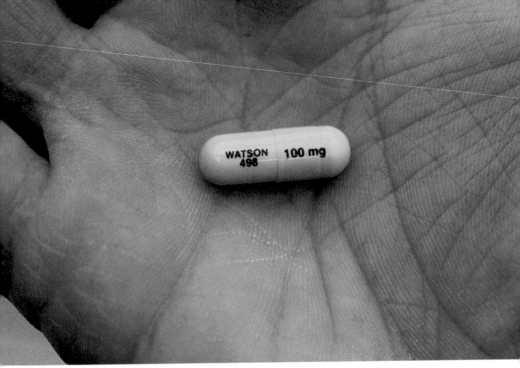

Some doctors treat people with chronic Lyme disease long term by prescribing antibiotics longer than is recommended by the IDSA.

Firm in its belief that extended treatment can be necessary in cases such as Weintraub's, in 2003 ILADS compiled its own set of "evidence-based" treatment guidelines to stand against the IDSA's. These guidelines advocate treatment length being based on clinical response—that is, if the patient appears to have fully recovered—rather than a preset number of weeks.

A Dangerous Solution?

Long-term antibiotic treatment is not without risks, however. In addition to targeting pathogens, antibiotics can also kill useful bacteria that live in the human digestive system. This can lead to yeast infections, which are fungal infections that affect the genitals, skin, or mouth. Antibiotics can also cause an inflammation of the bowels known as colitis, the symptoms of which include abdominal pain and bloody diarrhea.

Patients receiving extended intravenous therapy have developed inflammation of the gallbladder and gallstones, in some cases severe enough to require removal of the organ.

Allen Steere

Allen Steere, the man credited with discovering Lyme disease in the United States, is a professor of rheumatology at Harvard University. He has written over three hundred articles on the illness and is one of the doctors who created the treatment guidelines recommended by the Infectious Diseases Society of America.

Steere does not believe in the existence of chronic Lyme disease and believes in general that the disease is overdiagnosed and overtreated. "I suppose Lyme disease is one of the few diseases that some people want to have, because it's defined," he told the New York Times in 1999. "I think it's very difficult to have something that is not well understood."[1] He says he sees Lyme as a clear-cut disease, not one that produces a wide variety of vague symptoms, like some doctors believe.

Steere's position has made him an unpopular man among those in the Lyme community who insist chronic Lyme is real. His speaking engagements have been picketed, and he has been threatened with violence on several occasions. Steere has his supporters as well, however. According to world-famous violinist Itzhak Perlman, with whom Steere, also a violinist, once performed, "I have known Allen Steere for almost 40 years; he is an ethical, gentle, humble human being who happens to be an outstanding physician. . . . Shame on those who would threaten Dr. Steere. The very diagnosis they seek would have been unavailable, if not for him."[2]

1. Quoted in David France. "Scientist at Work: Allen C. Steere." New York Times, May 4, 1999. www.nytimes.com/1999/05/04/health/scientist-at-work-allen-c-steere-lyme-expert-developed-big-picture-of-tiny-tick.html?src=pm.
2. Itzhak Perlman. "Stalking Dr. Steere." New York Times, July 15, 2001. www.nytimes.com/2001/07/15/magazine/l-stalking-dr-steere-167843.html.

Other problems can arise from the system used to administer the intravenous medication. Patients on long-term intravenous therapy often have a special line called a catheter inserted beneath the skin in the chest area. This line leads through the chest tissue to a large vein, and the medication is delivered through the line into the vein. The presence of the line can cause blood clots in the body, and infections can also occur. According to Jonathan A. Edlow, one woman died from "massive fungal infection caused by an intravenous catheter that had been in place for more than two years so she could receive ceftriaxone for Lyme disease."[28]

Another concern is one that has been very much in the news in recent years—the concern that overuse of antibiotics

Lyme patients on long-term intravenous (IV) therapy have a catheter inserted in the chest area. The presence of the IV line can cause infections and blood clots.

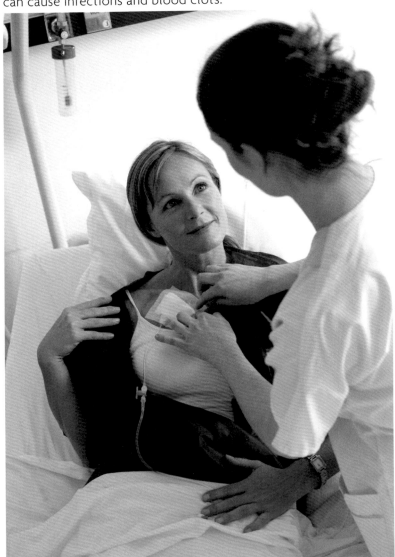

can lead to drug-resistant bacteria. Whenever a person takes an antibiotic, while many pathogens are destroyed, a few will resist the antibiotic and survive. These surviving bacteria can then multiply, passing on their antibiotic resistance to the new bacteria that are created. Thus, the next time an antibiotic is prescribed to cure an illness caused by that bacteria, it will be much less effective. Also, weaker bacteria can acquire genetic material from other antibiotic-resistant bacteria near them through various methods of transmission, which results in the weaker bacteria becoming antibiotic-resistant as well. This process has led to the death of at least one person being treated for Lyme, a fifty-two-year-old woman in Minnesota who died in 2009 after she developed a drug-resistant strain of bacteria after being treated with antibiotics for ten weeks.

The Case Against Extended Treatment

In addition to these worries about the medical complications that can develop from an overuse of antibiotics, doctors who do not believe in chronic Lyme state other reasons that long-term treatment is not a logical solution. In cases where patients report improvement in their symptoms after extended antibiotic treatment, the IDSA says this could be due to one of three reasons: (1) the patient has a strong mental belief that the treatment will help, so they perceive their symptoms have improved; this is known as the placebo effect; (2) antibiotics do help reduce inflammation in many cases, which can lead to an improvement in some symptoms; or (3) the person in fact had another illness besides Lyme that responded positively to the antibiotics. These doctors point to clinical trials that they say prove no benefit to prolonged treatment. (ILADS members say these trials had serious design flaws, and that one of them was even halted halfway through.)

Critics of long-term treatment also point to the cost to patients. According to Phillip Baker, one of the doctors involved with three of the clinical trials, extended therapy can cost a person as much as fifty thousand dollars a year. He believes doctors who advocate for this treatment are taking advantage

Extended therapy can cost a person thousands of dollars a year in medical bills.

of patients. According to him, "the net result is that people are paying a lot of money for something that's not doing them much good."[29]

Disbelievers in chronic Lyme also feel that doctors who treat long term are sometimes themselves the cause of a patient's worsening symptoms. Rheumatologist Leonard Sigal explains: "It is the psychological burden . . . induced by the suggestion that these patients are chronically ill, maybe forever—that causes them to assume a sick role they can never escape. It's a terrible thing to do to a patient."[30] Sigal believes when a patient does not respond to the usual antibiotic treatment and is told by a Lyme-literate doctor that he or she will need many more years of it, this can have a profound effect on the person's mental state. As he puts it:

> "Doc, are you telling me you can't cure this, that I'm stuck with these spirochetes crawling around in my head?" If

I really believed that about myself, I don't think I'd be a happy camper at all. I would be very upset, extraordinarily stressed out, and I wouldn't be surprised if whatever symptoms I had were remarkably worsened. And probably joined by new symptoms.[31]

Caught in the middle of the debate are the patients, who sometimes do not know whom to believe. Brian Ebner of Madison, Wisconsin, was ill for eleven years and saw twenty-four doctors before finally visiting one who diagnosed him with Lyme. The doctor prescribed long-term treatment that included Ebner taking 106 pills a day. Despite following the doctor's instructions, Ebner had his doubts. "It's hard to figure out what's going on," he said. "It's just crushing. On the one hand you've got your traditional family doctor who says all you need is one month of antibiotics and you're done, and on the other end of the spectrum you have these Lyme-literate persons throwing everything against the wall to see what sticks."[32]

Lawsuits and Legislation

The battle over the existence of chronic Lyme disease is increasingly being fought in the country's courthouses and boardrooms. Several Lyme-literate doctors have been investigated by state medical boards after being accused of misdiagnosing patients with Lyme disease, causing them harm through treatment procedures, or failing to uphold certain standards of care.

One of the more well-known accused has been Connecticut's Charles Ray Jones, an expert on pediatric Lyme disease. In 2010 the eighty-one-year-old Jones was accused of prescribing medication for a child he had not met and ordering blood and urine tests for patients before seeing them, among other things. Jones countered that he merely continued a prescription for the child of a nurse he knew well and trusted, and that he ordered the blood and urine tests in advance because he had a six-month wait time to see new patients. After paying a fine and agreeing to have someone monitor his practice, Jones was put on probation but allowed to keep his license.

The other side of the Lyme dispute has struck legal blows as well. In 2006 Connecticut attorney general Richard Blumenthal launched an investigation of the IDSA panel that created the Lyme treatment guidelines. One of the more serious accusations Blumenthal made was that certain doctors on the panel were also paid consultants for insurance companies. This could be considered a serious conflict of interest, because if the IDSA did recommend long-term antibiotic treatment for Lyme disease, insurance companies would likely be required to pay for it. Thus, from a financial standpoint it would seem to make sense that these companies would not want the IDSA to advise long-term treatment and might pressure their consultants on the guidelines panel to speak against it. A spokesperson for the IDSA, however, denied that any of the panel members benefited financially from the content of the guidelines.

In 2008 Connecticut attorney general Richard Blumenthal and the IDSA agreed to review the guidelines for long-term treatment of Lyme disease.

In 2008 Blumenthal and the IDSA agreed to a review of the guidelines by a new panel, and ultimately the guidelines were upheld. The review panel's report, issued in 2010, states: "The risk/benefit ratio from prolonged antibiotic therapy strongly discourages prolonged antibiotic courses for Lyme disease. . . . Only high-quality, prospective, controlled clinical trial data demonstrating both benefit and safety will be sufficient to change the current recommendations."[33] This ruling caused much anger and dismay in the Lyme-literate community. Pat Smith, president of the nonprofit Lyme Disease Association, issued a statement critical of the review panel:

Connecticut governor M. Jodi Rell signed a state law providing protection to doctors who prescribe long-term antibiotic treatments to Lyme patients.

They admit to receiving a large volume of case reports and case series that attested to "perceived" clinical improvement with long term treatment. One would assume in most cases, doctors were perceiving the improvement in patients and thus their years of clinical judgment would carry significant weight. Yet they excluded all of that evidence as not justified.[34]

Believers in chronic Lyme have won some critical legal support, however. In 2010, a state law was passed in Massachusetts providing protection to doctors who prescribe long-term antibiotic treatment to Lyme patients. Connecticut, Rhode Island, and California have similar laws. M. Jodi Rell, the governor of Connecticut, issued a press release at the time of that state's passage of the bill, stating: "Doctors in Connecticut—the absolute epicenter of Lyme disease—can continue to do what is best for their patients suffering from this complex illness. . . . The bill also recognizes that Lyme disease patients must have the freedom to choose what remedy or regimen best meets their needs."[35]

It seems unlikely that the uproar over chronic Lyme will fade any time in the near future, and more legal battles are sure to arise. Until a test is developed that can identify without a doubt the presence of *B. burgdorferi* bacteria in a person claiming to have chronic Lyme, the controversy over its existence and how—or even if—to treat it will continue. "It's like two people speaking different languages and trying to communicate," as Kenneth Liegner of ILADS says. "It's very nasty, very destructive."[36]

CHAPTER FIVE

Prevention and the Future of Lyme

Currently, as the study of Lyme disease continues and medical researchers attempt to discover new and better ways to deal with the illness, the best treatment is simply not to get infected in the first place. There are precautions that an individual can take if planning to venture into an area that may be infected with ticks. Additionally, more wide-reaching efforts have been made to reduce the dangers faced by residents of tick-infested areas.

Deer-Reduction Methods

Many Lyme experts believe that reducing the number of ticks in a particular area can greatly lower the risk of people getting infected. Some communities have attempted to do this by reducing the number of deer—one of the primary food sources for adult ticks—in the region. This can be successful because adult deer in urban environments tend to stay within their own home range and do not migrate into areas where deer have been removed. Deer reduction can be carried out by hiring licensed sharpshooters, allowing regulated hunting, or holding controlled hunts. According to the Connecticut Department of Public Health, controlled hunts carried out between 1996 and 2004 in Groton, Connecticut, that reduced the deer population from seventy-seven deer per square mile (2.59 sq. km) to ten per square mile, also resulted in an 83 percent reduction in Lyme disease incidents among residents.

Other methods of deer reduction that do not involve killing the deer have been researched but found to be less effective. One approach involved fertility control, in which deer would be shot with a dart containing a birth control agent. This method was found to be effective only in very small, isolated deer populations, however, and was extremely costly. Another option that has been explored is trapping and relocating deer, but this is also very expensive and can result in the spread of disease from one deer herd to another. Additionally, this is very stressful on the deer, and many die due to the experience.

One small-scale practice that has had some success is fencing. This is only suitable for a very restricted area, however, such as an individual's house and yard. Ultrasonic devices are now available, as well, which detect motion and then produce sound waves that are unpleasant to deer.

Controlled deer hunts in Groton, Connecticut, performed between 1996 and 2004 resulted in an 83 percent reduction in Lyme disease incidents among residents.

Targeting the Ticks

Other attempts to reduce the number of ticks in a particular area focus on killing the ticks themselves. One method recommended by the American Lyme Disease Foundation is the four-poster bait station. The bait station has a central bin filled with corn and a feeding station at either end. When deer eat the corn, their ears rub against rollers mounted on the feeding stations. These rollers are coated in pesticide that kills any ticks attached to the deer's ears, head, neck, and shoulders. As the deer grooms itself, it spreads the pesticide onto other parts of its body as well. A similar bait station has been developed that places a collar treated with tick pesticide around the deer's neck as it feeds.

An Agricultural Experiment Station worker sweeps the edge of a yard for ticks.

Another option is a system that targets the ticks that feed on mice, which are a primary carrier of Lyme disease. Special "tick tubes," which contain cotton that has been treated with a pesticide that kills ticks, are placed in areas frequented by mice. Mice take this cotton to build their nests, and the pesticide helps eliminate ticks in their larval and nymphal stages while leaving the mice unharmed. A system called Maxforce Tick Management, which treated mice with an anti-tick pesticide much like the way the popular Frontline flea-and-tick control treats dogs and cats, was in use briefly but the manufacturer discontinued the product in 2006 after reports that squirrels were chewing through the Maxforce boxes and exposing the pesticide to children and non-target animals.

Some people treat their yards with pesticides to reduce the tick population. It is recommended that spray be applied once in the late spring or early summer to control tick nymphs, with a second application in October to target adult ticks. The pesticide should be sprayed on tick habitat areas only, such as ground cover shrubs near the house or walkways and areas where the lawn meets the woods. Several yards beyond the woodland border should also be treated, as this is where a high concentration of ticks can usually be found.

Other techniques that can be used to reduce tick numbers around a home include placing a barrier such as wood chips or gravel in between the edge of the yard and the woodlands, mowing the lawn frequently, and clearing away leaf litter and brush.

Personal Precautions

There are also steps individuals can take to protect themselves against being bitten by ticks when walking or playing outdoors. While it is best to stay clear of tick-infested areas altogether, if this is not possible a person should avoid contact with leaf litter and overgrown vegetation and walk in the center of woodland trails.

Clothing should be light in color, so any ticks that attach to it will be easily visible. Long pants, long-sleeved shirts, and

Famous Faces of Lyme

Several well-known people have been infected with Lyme disease. For example, Daryl Hall of the musical duo Hall and Oates was diagnosed with Lyme in 2005 after he fell following a concert and spent the next three days in bed. He said he still had recurring symptoms three years after contracting and being treated for the disease.

Rebecca Wells, author of the best-selling novel *Divine Secrets of the Ya-Ya Sisterhood,* was ill for five years before being correctly diagnosed with Lyme. Amy Tan, author of the best-selling novel *The Joy Luck Club,* was also sick for years before being diagnosed with Lyme. Lyme has affected several actors and actresses, such as Richard Gere, Parker Posey, and Jamie-Lynn Sigler, and sports figures, including pro golfer Tim Simpson and runner Bart Yasso.

Several prominent politicians have also had brushes with Lyme. New York senator Charles Schumer was bitten by a tick in 2007 while on an upstate tour of dams and noticed a bull's-eye rash shortly after. Former New York governor George Pataki and former New Jersey governor Christie Todd Whitman were both treated for Lyme disease. Even George W. Bush received treatment during his presidency when it was discovered he had a telltale EM rash.

Former New Jersey governor Christie Todd Whitman talks to the press about her Lyme disease at a press conference in 1996.

hats are recommended, and long hair should be tied back. Pants can be tucked into socks and shirts tucked into pants to provide fewer entry points for ticks to reach the skin. Shoes that cover the entire foot should always be worn.

A person can also use insect repellent. One that contains 20 percent DEET (the most common active ingredient in such repellents) can be applied to both bare skin and clothing. Because DEET is a powerful toxin, it should not be applied near the eyes or nose or to broken skin or skin covered by clothing. Users should also be careful not to inhale DEET. DEET works by turning off receptors on the tick's antenna that it uses to detect the presence of a human. Another chemical, permethrin, which kills ticks on contact, can be applied to clothing but not to skin.

Upon returning from a tick-infested area, a person should do a thorough check for ticks, using a mirror to examine hard-to-see areas such as the armpits, scalp, backs of the knees, and groin. Clothing should be checked before entering the home and then washed in hot water and dried on high heat for at least thirty minutes.

If an attached tick is found on a person, certain steps should be taken to ensure its safe removal. Using fine-tipped tweezers, grab the tick as close to the skin as possible. Gentle pressure should then be used to pull the tick straight up from the skin, without any twisting, jerking, or crushing of the tick's body. Commercial tools specifically designed for removing ticks are also available, and a study of three such tools conducted at Ohio State University showed them to be more effective at removing tick nymphs than regular tweezers. The hands should be washed immediately after removing the tick, and the site of the bite cleaned with soap and water or an antiseptic. Methods such as applying petroleum jelly or nail polish to the tick, or burning it with a match, should not be attempted, as they can cause the tick to discharge saliva—and therefore possibly bacteria—into the skin.

The person should then monitor the site of the bite for a rash and notify a doctor if one appears, or if fever, headache,

Insect repellents that contain 20 percent DEET have been found to be effective in warding off ticks.

and fatigue occur. If the tick was discovered very shortly after exposure, however, it is highly unlikely the person will become infected with Lyme, even if the tick was carrying *B. burgdorferi* bacteria.

The Search for a Vaccine

Precautions such as these will be necessary until science can discover a better way to protect the population against Lyme disease, such as development of a vaccine. A vaccine is a preparation of living or dead microorganisms injected into the body that causes the immune system to act against that particular microorganism. The person does not get sick from this injection, because the microorganisms are either dead or too weak to cause any harm, but their mere presence still provokes the production of antibodies against them. Then the next time a person is exposed to that microorganism, the body will already have antibodies stored against it, and the illness will be wiped out before the person feels any effects from it.

Although there is currently no Lyme vaccine available for humans, one was briefly on the market. The three-dose vaccine was called LYMErix, and it was produced by a company called GlaxoSmithKlein. LYMErix was approved by the U.S. Food and Drug Administration (FDA) in 1998, but by 2000 federal health authorities were investigating claims that it was causing severe cases of arthritis in some people, and in others possibly causing old, previously treated infections of Lyme to flare up again. Allen Steere, who directed GlaxoSmithKlein's trials of the vaccine, said that even though he recommended its passage, the vaccine had the potential to cause an autoimmune reaction in persons with a certain genetic marker, and this reaction could result in treatment-resistant arthritis. The FDA approved the vaccine anyway, and, even after the claims that it was making people sick began rolling in, left it on the market while it attempted to determine if the vaccine was indeed the cause of the problems. Eventually, the FDA stated it could find no compelling evidence LYMErix was unsafe. GlaxoSmithKlein

A sign advises hikers of the proper clothing to wear when in a tick-infested area. Light-colored long pants, long-sleeved shirts, hats, and long, thick socks are recommended.

stopped manufacturing the vaccine in 2002, however, claiming they were doing so due to poor sales.

The vaccine was created using one of the Lyme bacteria's outer proteins, outer surface protein A, to provoke the body's immune response. Since LYMErix's failure, scientists have been seeking other ways to use this protein without the unfortunate side effects that were reported with LYMErix. Another protein, outer surface protein C, is also being examined as a possible candidate for developing a new vaccine.

Other approaches are being researched as well. Scientists at Yale University are studying the possibility of creating a vaccine that would target the tick itself as it feeds on a vaccinated person. They discovered that a protein present in tick saliva called tick histamine release factor, was helping to transmit *B. burgdorferi* from tick to person. Studies done in mice thus far have shown that blocking this protein cuts down on the efficiency of the tick's feeding and has resulted in fewer Lyme spirochetes being transmitted to the mice.

Researchers at the Centers for Disease Control and Prevention (CDC) have been focusing on a gene activated by the Lyme bacteria during tick feeding that is necessary to transmit infection. They altered the bacteria to disable this gene and then injected the altered bacteria into mice and allowed ticks to feed on them. Next, they took fifteen healthy mice and allowed the ticks that had fed on the infected mice to feed on the healthy mice. Only two of the fifteen mice contracted Lyme. The researchers hope to use the knowledge learned from this and other experiments involving this gene to develop a Lyme vaccine.

Other New Advances

In addition to a vaccine, scientists continue to search for more reliable serological tests to aid in the diagnosis of Lyme. One such effort, the C6 ELISA (enzyme-linked immunosorbent assay), was developed by researchers at Tulane University and is said by some experts to be highly effective in detecting Lyme in its early stages, when the traditional two-tier ELISA/

Lyme and Pets

Pets can also be affected by Lyme disease. Dogs are most commonly the victims of the illness, although cats and other domestic animals such as horses and cattle can also become infected. Symptoms in dogs and cats commonly include fever, swelling in the joints, lameness, loss of appetite, swollen lymph nodes, and unusual drowsiness. Pets do not display the EM rash. If the disease is untreated, serious kidney problems can develop. A blood test may be used to diagnose the illness, but these are often unreliable, so many veterinarians will choose to go by the symptoms along with the animal's history and whether or not the area in which the animal lives has many cases of Lyme. Lyme in pets is treated with antibiotics.

Although there are vaccines against Lyme available for cats and dogs, many veterinarians do not believe they are very effective and do not recommend them. Tick control is important, and chemicals that kill insects (insecticides) applied to the skin of pets is a common method of preventing bites. Avoiding taking pets to areas with large numbers of ticks and checking pets for ticks frequently are also highly recommended.

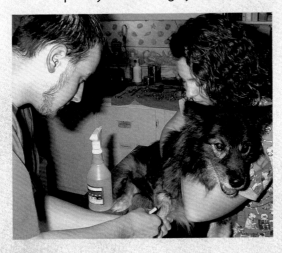

A dog is given an antibiotic treatment for Lyme disease. Dogs—as well as cats, horses, and cattle—can become infected and die from the disease.

Western blot process can often fail. The C6 ELISA detects antibodies to the C6 peptide found in *B. burgdorferi.* (A peptide is a compound made up of two or more amino acids, which are the building blocks of proteins.) According to Mario Philipp of Tulane:

> The C6 peptide is part of a lipoprotein, VlsE, which sits on the surface membrane of the spirochete. Parts of this protein are changed by the spirochete as it infects the host, but other portions, C6 included, stay constant and stimulate an early and strong antibody response. This is why the C6 test is so sensitive, as it detects antibody very early in the infection.[37]

The C6 ELISA can also detect European as well as North American strains of *B. burgdorferi.* Some support exists for the C6 ELISA as a stand-alone test to replace the ELISA/Western blot combination, but other scientists worry about the number of false positives the test can produce, and they say more research is needed.

Also being studied for usefulness in diagnosing Lyme is the luciferase immunoprecipitation system (LIPS) test. This type of test has been used to detect viral and fungal infections for a few years, but only recently have scientists begun to try to detect antibody responses to Lyme bacteria with it. In June 2010 Lyme researchers at the National Institutes of Health reported impressive results using LIPS and expressed the opinion that those results marked LIPS as an efficient method of evaluating antibody responses in Lyme patients.

Further progress in better understanding Lyme was made in 2010 when researchers at the Stony Brook University Medical Center in New York successfully mapped the genetic blueprint of thirteen strains of Lyme-causing bacteria. This work could potentially impact all aspects of how the disease is handled. Benjamin Luft, the study's senior author, states: "By characterizing every gene in the Lyme disease agents family, we have a blueprint of every possible characteristic of the organism. This is the building block to developing more accurate and effective diagnostic tests, therapeutic agents and vaccines."[38]

Research on Lyme disease will undoubtedly continue and most likely intensify in the upcoming years as more and more cases are reported annually and the controversial nature of the illness drives scientists to search for concrete answers. Joseph Jemsek, a physician in Washington, D.C., who specializes in treating Lyme patients, is optimistic about the future: "What I sense is that we're at the beginning of something that is going to be huge, just like I had that feeling twenty-some years ago with HIV [AIDS]. . . . It's going to be an explosive area of medicine and we're going to learn a lot about chronic illness, and I think that's going to help health care tremendously."[39]

Notes

Introduction: Danger in the Woods

1. Quoted in Lisa W. Foderaro. "For 3 with Lyme Disease, Pain Without End." *New York Times*, January 4, 1989. www.nytimes.com/1989/01/04/nyregion/for-3-with-lyme-disease-pain-without-end.html.
2. Polly Murray. *The Widening Circle*. New York: St. Martin's, 1996, p. 286.

Chapter One: What Is Lyme Disease?

3. Alan G. Barbour. *Lyme Disease: The Cause, the Cure, the Controversy*. Baltimore: Johns Hopkins University Press, 1996, p. 39.

Chapter Two: Symptoms

4. Quoted in Constance Bean. *Beating Lyme: Understanding and Treating This Often Complex and Misdiagnosed Disease*. New York: American Management Association, 2008, p. 74.
5. Quoted in "Bob's Story." Southwestern Wisconsin and Illinois Lyme Leagues. www.sewill.org/story3.htm.
6. Quoted in "Bob's Story."
7. Pamela Weintraub. *Cure Unknown: Inside the Lyme Epidemic*. New York: St. Martin's, 2008, p. 30.
8. Hilary McDonald. "Lyme Disease Is More than a Tick Bite." Lyme Alliance. http://web.archive.org/web/20021029214619/www.lymealliance.org/personal/archiveI/archiveI_5.php.
9. Quoted in P.J. Langhoff. *It's All in Your Head: Around the World in 80 Lyme Patient Stories*. Hustisford, WI: Allegory, 2007, p. 222.
10. Robert Bransfield. "The Neuropsychiatric Assessment of Lyme Disease." Mental Health and Illness. www.mentalhealthandillness.com/tnaold.html.

11. "A Long, Strange Trip: One Woman's Journey Through the Land of Lyme Disease." Lyme Alliance. http://web .archive.org/web/20021102143806/www.lymealliance.org/ personal/archiveV/archiveV_8.php.
12. "A Long, Strange Trip."
13. Quoted in *Under Our Skin*. Directed by Andy Abrams Wilson. Sausalito, CA: Open Eye Pictures, 2008.
14. Quoted in Bean. *Beating Lyme*, p. 217.
15. Weintraub. *Cure Unknown*, p. 170.

Chapter Three: Diagnosis and Treatment

16. Quoted in Jonathan A. Edlow. *Bull's Eye: Unraveling the Medical Mystery of Lyme*. New Haven, CT: Yale University Press, 2003, pp. 177–178.
17. Weintraub. *Cure Unknown*, p. 200.
18. Edlow. *Bull's Eye*, pp. 185–186.
19. Quoted in Patricia Callahan and Trine Tsouderos. "Some Chronic Lyme Disease Promoters Run Afoul of the Law." *Los Angeles Times*, December 27, 2010. www.latimes.com/ health/la-he-lyme-disease-side-20101227,0,6632899.story.

Chapter Four: The Aftermath of Infection

20. "Basic Information About Lyme Disease." International Lyme and Associated Diseases Society. www.ilads.org/ lyme_disease/about_lyme1.html.
21. Quoted in Frederik Joelving. "Few Docs Recognize 'Chronic' Lyme Disease." Medline Plus. www.nlm.nih.gov/ medlineplus/news/fullstory_104718.html.
22. Jentri Anders. "B-flats." Lyme Alliance. http://web.archive .org/web/20020816114438/www.lymealliance.org/personal/ archiveV/archiveV_6.php.
23. Quoted in Jane Gross. "In Lyme Disease Debate, Some Patients Feel Lost." *New York Times*, July 7, 2001. www .nytimes.com/2001/07/07/nyregion/in-lyme-disease-debate-some-patients-feel-lost.html.
24. Quoted in Mary Carmichael. "The Great Lyme Debate." *Newsweek*, August 6, 2007. www.newsweek.com/ 2007/ 08/05/the-great-lyme-debate.html.

25. Quoted in "Faces of Lyme Disease." Lyme Disease Foundation. www.lyme.org/turley.html.
26. Quoted in Amanda Korman. "Two Sides of a Disease." International Lyme and Associated Diseases Society, October 10, 2010. www.ilads.org/news/lyme_news/80.html.
27. Weintraub. *Cure Unknown*, p. 291.
28. Edlow. *Bull's Eye*, p. 213.
29. Quoted in Claudia Kalb. "Lyme Time in D.C.: Unraveling How to Best Treat the Disease." *Newsweek*, July 30, 2009. www.newsweek.com/blogs/the-human-condition/2009/07/30/lyme-time-in-d-c-unraveling-how-to-best-treat-the-disease.html.
30. Quoted in Weintraub. *Cure Unknown*, p. 128.
31. Quoted in Weintraub. *Cure Unknown*, p. 129.
32. Quoted in Shawn Doherty. "Dispute Spreads on How to Treat Lyme." *Madison (WI) Capital Times*, June 30, 2010. http://host.madison.com/ct/news/local/health_med_fit/article_57d2f978-83c2-11df-bf04-001cc4c002e0.html.
33. "Final Report of the Lyme Disease Review Panel of the Infectious Diseases Society of America (IDSA)." Infectious Diseases Society of America. www.idsociety.org/Content.aspx?id=16520.
34. Pat Smith. "Statement of the National Non Profit Lyme Disease Association, Inc. on the IDSA Guidelines Panel Decision 4-22-10." April 23, 2010. www.lymedisease association.org/index.php?option=com_content&view=article&id=616:idsa-guidelines-panel-decision-4-22-10&catid=7:conflict-report&Itemid=398.
35. "Governor Rell Signs Bill That Shields Doctors in Treatment of Lyme Disease." CT.gov. June 22, 2009. www.ct.gov/governorrell/cwp/view.asp?A=3675&Q=442100.
36. Quoted in Gary Santaniello. "Lyme Disease Divide." *Hartford (CT) Courant*, September 17, 2006. http://articles.courant.com/2006-09-17/features/0609150349_1_lyme-disease-corkscrew-shaped-bacterium-lyme-bacterium.

Chapter Five: Prevention and the Future of Lyme

37 Quoted in Denise Lang. *Coping with Lyme Disease: A Practical Guide to Dealing with Diagnosis and Treatment.* New York: Holt, 2004, pp. 58–59.

38. "Genetic Blueprint of Bacteria Causing Lyme Disease Unraveled." Stony Brook University Physicians. October 13, 2010. www.stonybrookphysicians.com/html_community/news_view.asp?item=316.

39. Quoted in Wilson, *Under Our Skin.*

Glossary

antibody: Any of a large number of proteins produced by specialized white cells in response to the appearance of an antigen that act against that antigen in an immune response.

antigen: Any substance foreign to the body that causes an immune response.

bacteria: Extremely small single-celled organisms. Many kinds of bacteria are harmless, but some can cause disease.

chronic: Long lasting or recurrent.

endemic: Constantly present to a greater degree in that area than in others.

fatigue: Physical or mental weariness.

immune response: The body's response to an antigen that occurs when white blood cells identify the antigen as foreign (not belonging) and begin the formation of antibodies and other cells capable of reacting with the antigen and making it harmless.

inflammation: A way in which the body reacts to infection, usually characterized by redness, swelling, warmth, and pain.

insomnia: An inability to sleep.

Lyme-literate: A descriptive term for a doctor who treats large numbers of Lyme cases, usually with prolonged courses of antibiotics.

malaise: A general feeling of physical discomfort.

nymph: The third stage in the life cycle of a tick. Nymphs are extremely tiny—about the size of a poppy seed—and are responsible for most cases of Lyme disease transmission.

pathogens: Specific agents, such as viruses or bacteria, that cause a disease.

reservoir: A passive host in which an organism that causes sickness in some other species lives and multiplies, usually without damaging the host.

serological tests: Tests that examine a person's blood serum for antibodies to a particular pathogen.

spirochete: Any member of an order of bacteria characterized by a long spiral shape, many of which cause illness.

vector: An organism that transmits a bacterium or virus that causes a disease to another organism.

zoonosis: A disease that can be passed from animals to humans.

Organizations to Contact

American Lyme Disease Foundation (ALDF)

PO Box 466
Lyme, CT 06371
Website: www.aldf.com

This organization is dedicated to the prevention, diagnosis, and treatment of Lyme disease and seeks to educate the public about the illness.

Centers for Disease Control and Prevention (CDC)

1600 Clifton Rd.
Atlanta, GA 30333
Phone: (800) 232-4636
Website: www.cdc.gov

The CDC seeks to prevent and control diseases, injuries, and disabilities. It also provides health information to medical professionals and the public.

Infectious Diseases Society of America (IDSA)

1300 Wilson Blvd., Ste. 300
Arlington, VA 22209
Phone: (703) 299-0200 • Fax: (703) 299-0204
Website: www.idsociety.org

The IDSA is an organization of health-care professionals who specialize in infectious diseases such as Lyme. It seeks to improve patient care and foster education and research on infectious diseases.

International Lyme and Associated Diseases Society (ILADS)

PO Box 341461
Bethesda, MD
Phone: (301) 263-1080
Website: www.ilads.org

ILADS is a nonprofit medical society dedicated to the diagnosis and appropriate treatment of Lyme disease. Many of its directors and officers are Lyme-literate doctors.

Lyme Disease Association (LDA)

PO Box 1438
Jackson, NJ 08527
Phone: (888) 366-6611 • Fax: (732) 938-215
Website: www.LymeDiseaseAssociation.org

The LDA funds research on Lyme and seeks to educate the public about the disease.

For More Information

Books

Constance Bean. *Beating Lyme: Understanding and Treating This Often Complex and Misdiagnosed Disease*. New York: American Management Association, 2008. This book covers all aspects of Lyme disease.

Jonathan A. Edlow. *Bull's Eye: Unraveling the Medical Mystery of Lyme*. New Haven, CT: Yale University Press, 2003. Edlow's book explores the discovery of Lyme disease in the United States. More suitable for older children.

Mark P. Friedlander Jr. *Outbreak: Disease Detectives at Work*. Minneapolis, MN: Twenty-First Century, 2009. This book introduces young readers to the study of disease occurrences in populations. One chapter focuses on Lyme.

Mary Wall. *Lyme Disease Is No Fun: Let's Get Well!* Jackson, NJ: Lyme Disease Association, 2004. This book is written for children suffering from Lyme and focuses on helping them understand the illness and how best to cope with it.

Pamela Weintraub. *Cure Unknown: Inside the Lyme Epidemic*. New York: St. Martin's, 2008. Recommended for older children, this book provides an in-depth look at the controversy over the existence of chronic Lyme.

Periodicals

Jane Gross. "In Lyme Disease Debate, Some Patients Feel Lost." *New York Times*, July 7, 2001.

Russ Juskalian. "My Father's Mystery Illness." *Newsweek*, August 24, 2010.

Websites

Lyme Disease (http://faculty.washington.edu/chudler/lyme.html). This website maintained by science teacher Lynn Bleeker provides basic information about Lyme disease.

"Lyme Disease," Centers for Disease Control and Prevention (www.cdc.gov/ncidod/dvbid/lyme). This site provides general information about the transmission and treatment of Lyme disease, along with statistics of reported cases and informational guides and brochures.

"Lyme Disease," TeensHealth.org (http://kidshealth.org/teen/infections/skin_rashes/lyme_disease.html). This site gives an overview of Lyme disease and its symptoms, treatment, and prevention.

Index

Picture Credits

About the Author

Shannon Kelly lives in New York City and is employed in the entertainment business. In addition to her full-time job, she has also worked as a copy editor and development editor on a number of reference books over the last decade. In her spare time, she enjoys photography, traveling, and watching medical shows on television.